THE HIDDEN WORLD

To Sue, my wife,
and our Jeromy and Gigi,
gratefully and lovingly

ACKNOWLEDGEMENTS

It was Norman Potter's striking and perceptive photographs, originally commissioned for a series of videotape programmes, that prompted the writing of this book. My first debt of gratitude goes to him.

Next I wish to record my deep appreciation to those many people who comprise the Foundation that bears my name, and who over the years have so generously shared with me their knowledge and experience. It is to them that I dedicate this book, in acknowledgement of all that I owe them. Indeed but for them there would have been no book to write.

Michael Humfrey has read the successive versions of the script and patiently helped and advised me throughout. John Bright-Holmes, Dr Anne Hamilton, MRCP, Hampden Inskip, QC, Sir Christopher Foxley-Norris, GCB, DSO, Gillian Corney and Christopher MacLehose have also given me invaluable help. Eileen Amiel typed and retyped what must have seemed a constantly changing text. I thank them all very warmly.

I cannot end without mentioning my family who supported me in more ways than they know, and who good-humouredly put up with even more absent-mindedness than usual.

L.C.

CONTENTS

ILLUSTRATIONS

Photographs by Norman Potter

between pages 96–7

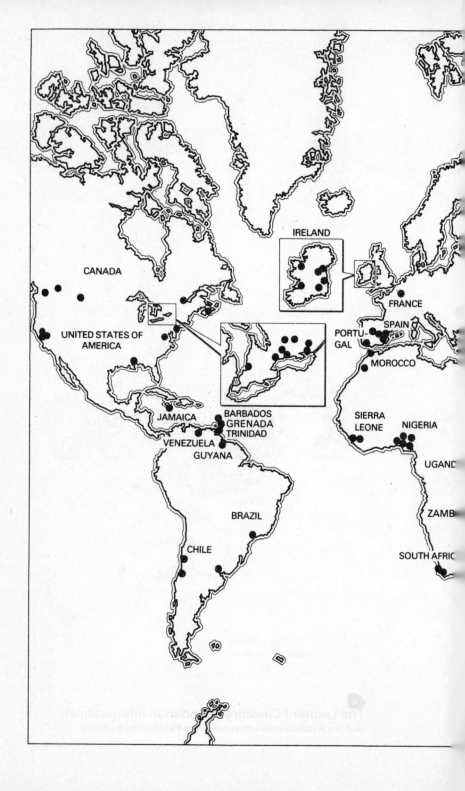

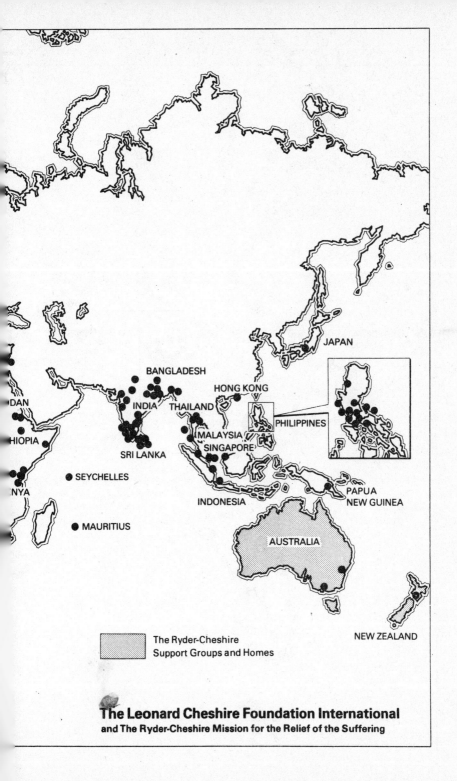

JAPAN

BANGLADESH

HONG KONG

INDIA   THAILAND

DAN

PHILIPPINES

HIOPIA

MALAYSIA
SINGAPORE

SRI LANKA

● SEYCHELLES

NYA

PAPUA
NEW GUINEA

INDONESIA

● MAURITIUS

AUSTRALIA

The Ryder-Cheshire
Support Groups and Homes

NEW ZEALAND

The Leonard Cheshire Foundation International
and The Ryder-Cheshire Mission for the Relief of the Suffering

Chapter One

PERSONAL ENCOUNTER

It all began for me very innocently, with a telephone call. At that particular stage in my life, thirty years ago, the telephone did not ring very often and when it did it seldom boded any good. Either a creditor was asking when he could expect to receive his money, or some new complication had arisen in the arrangements that I was being forced to make for the sale of an estate. This call was to prove unlike any other that I had ever received.

A pleasant voice announced the matron of the hospital at Petersfield, and said that Mr Arthur Dykes, with whom she understood I was acquainted, was lying in hospital suffering from an advanced stage of cancer. It would be helpful, said the matron, if I could come to see her.

I might have been excused for being slow on the uptake, for quite apart from the general worry and confusion of the situation in which I found myself, I had known the man not as 'Mr Dykes' but simply as Arthur, and I had not really known him very well at that. Moreover, I felt that there were enough problems to life as it was without adding this new one. I put on the best face I could, however, and agreed to call at the hospital the following morning.

The problems to which I refer were admittedly of my own creation, the result of having embarked upon a project which, though well intentioned, was unrealistic. At the end of the war I had retired from the Air Force, filled with I do not know how many different and confused ideas about what to do with my life. The totality of the war, which had cost fifty-five million lives, had impressed upon me the urgency of ensuring that such a catastrophe never happen again. But, how to do it? No one seemed to know; indeed, many did not seem even to worry. The war had been won, the aggressor defeated, and the time had come to settle down to the fulfilment of domestic goals.

In the pages that follow I want to present a picture of the world that has been my life for the past thirty-three years, the world of disabled people. It may seem a strange thing that in one breath I should talk about wanting to share in the struggle to prevent a third world war, and in the next say that my life's work had lain amongst disabled people. I do not have a ready answer, other than to recount my story as it has happened. The truth is that the sense of urgency about ensuring peace which I felt at the end of the war has never left me, and yet I know that it is in the world of disabled people that my life lies.

When I use the term 'world', I do not mean to separate disabled people from the rest of mankind, for that would be to contradict the basis of what I am setting out to say. Rather, I use it as indicating the sum of everything that affects disabled people as a consequence of their disability, whether in respect of their daily living, their material or spiritual needs, their inner longings and frustrations, their relationships with other people, their contribution to the well-being of their fellow men – whatever it might be.

This world into which I invite the reader is a world of many surprises, rich with human attainment and inner happiness, and as often the reverse, and yet it is a world that even to this day is little known and poorly understood. This is true to such an extent that I have come to think of it as a 'hidden world', hidden in the sense that few of us realize how many disabled persons there are within our own neighbourhood, let alone the world over, but hidden also in the sense that very few understand the true nature of the problem that disabled people face.

Today, in the so-called developed countries at least, disability has become almost an election issue. There is a great deal spoken and written about it; government measures are taken and statements of policy issued; a wealth of private organizations has sprung up, concerned with helping disabled people towards greater independence and self-fulfilment, or publicizing a particular aspect of their predicament or unacknowledged rights. There are many theorists and planners researching ideal solutions, laying down standards, analysing the attitudes of those doing the practical work in the field; and now, to help usher in a new era, the United Nations has declared 1981 'International Year of Disabled People'. To anyone who knew the situation thirty years ago, when very little was known about disability and those who suffered from it, the change that has come about in so short a time is remarkable indeed. But despite all that has happened, disabled people are still only imperfectly understood. They are still the subject of many misconceptions, even prejudice, and of much unacceptable generalization. They live intermingled with the rest of us, part and parcel of our human society at every level, and yet many of them in a world of their own, apart in a very real sense. With good reason we can talk of the world in which they live as a hidden one.

As I write, however, I have to acknowledge that what I have asserted of others may also be true of myself; that I too may have not properly understood the disabled person, or if I have that I shall not succeed in portraying a true and balanced picture of the world that we are about to enter. I lay no pretensions to any greater perceptiveness or insight than the next man working in the same field, and am fully conscious of the many times over these years that I have had to revise and reshape my thinking. I am very conscious too that it is above everything else with people that I have to do, with individual human beings, each a person in his own right, unique and unrepeatable, each a member of our human family destined for the same eternal end, with all the dignity and responsibility that this implies. They are people of every conceivable race and culture; very poor and very rich, old and young, and every possible gradation between, and are to be found amongst us wherever we happen to live, some our own kith and kin, others on the other side of the world with a life-style and pattern of thought very different indeed from ours.

That I was soon to become involved with them, at times sharing their own way of life, arose directly out of the experience of war. Heaven knows, I never wanted to go to war. I had grown up in the aftermath of World War I and often used to think about the men in the trenches. How any human being could endure what they endured, and still put the cause for which they were fighting before themselves, was beyond my comprehension. Also beyond my comprehension was the need for having to resort to war to settle international disputes. The very thought of it repelled me and, I think, frightened me, for I could not picture how I myself would manage under gunfire. But mine was the generation dominated by Hitler, and once he had shown himself in his true colours everything changed. The world that had looked so secure, so full of beauty and of promise, suddenly held a deadly enemy, and until he was brought under control there would be neither peace nor freedom in Europe.

It was the wartime RAF that gave a direction and a discipline to my life, and taught me that professionalism and team-work are the prerequisites of all human achievement. There I was shown what men and women can achieve when they are united in pursuit of a common goal clearly identified as just and good, and which they know they must attain at all costs. This feeling of solidarity, of all being in the same boat, transcending all divisions of race or class, dominated my post-war thinking, and convinced me that, if only we could retain our national sense of purpose and be well led, world peace might be attainable.

My thoughts, however, were ill-formed. No one I could find seemed able to crystallize them or put forward any realistic suggestion, and I myself could not think what to do with my life. By the spring of 1946 I had grown tired of theoretical discussions (which in any case were often beyond me), and so I took refuge in action. On a sudden impulse I suggested the formation of a community scheme for ex-servicemen like myself who had not succeeded in finding their niche in civilian life. The idea was a community where, by pooling our resources and such skills as we had acquired in the services, we would help with the rebuilding of post-war Britain and, at the same time, recapture something of the sense of purpose and comradeship which we appeared to have lost.

The proposal received a good press and an unexpectedly warm response from the public. With a minimal outlay of capital we were able to acquire two large properties, one of which was Le Court, near Liss in Hampshire, a three-hundred-acre estate on which stood a twenty-five-bedroomed Victorian house and thirty-two cottages. For all its early promise the scheme soon ran into difficulties, principally because its basic concept was unrealistic, and within eighteen months it was closed down, leaving a substantial legacy of debts. It was in the middle of this painful process of winding up the community's affairs and selling the Le Court Estate piece by piece to pay off the creditors that the telephone rang with its unexpected request.

Matron's point was simple enough. Hers was a cottage hospital with only two dozen beds; there was a long waiting list of people needing treatment which would put most of them back on their feet. Arthur's illness was beyond the reach of further medical treatment and he needed only bed care for the short time until he died. Under these circumstances she could not possibly reserve a bed for him for what might be anything from four to twelve months, and therefore another place would have to be found for him.

Arthur had been the pig-man at Le Court. He liked working on his own, and one hardly ever saw him except at meal-times. He started work very early and returned very late. But now that I had occasion to think about it I remembered that he had served in the RAF as a nursing orderly in a fairly lowly rank. He had been too old for the RAF but, on his application form, had dropped his age by ten years and was accepted.

In those first post-war years, ex-servicemen were given

priority, particularly when it came to hospitalization or social help, and what was more the new National Health Service was now committed to caring for everyone in time of sickness. With the strings I thought that I could still pull in Air Force and other circles, I felt sure that I should soon find an alternative place for Arthur. But in this I was proved wrong.

At first, when negative answers began to arrive, I thought that I was not presenting the case in the right way. Then, as each door closed in turn, I began to feel a little desperate. Time was passing, Matron telephoned more and more often, and I was finding it increasingly difficult to know what to say to Arthur. There were, of course, private nursing homes that would have taken him in, but these cost anything from £10 a week, and Arthur's only income was his National Assistance Allowance of 27s. 6d. per week. The County Medical Officer of Health, the ex-service organizations and the various hospitals to which I had been referred, had all answered with a polite but firm 'Sorry, but we can't help'. The reason, almost invariably, was that if there were nothing more to be done for Arthur from a medical point of view, they could not spare a bed.

On my first visit to the hospital, Matron told me that I was on no account to give Arthur the slightest hint that his cancer was incurable and that he was dying. I have to admit that I was rather thankful for this instruction. Although during the war, like so many other Commanding Officers, I had had the sad task of writing countless letters informing relatives of the death in action of a son or a husband, and had seen so much death and destruction, I had never been obliged to tell a man face to face that he was dying. The thought that I might now have to do so threw me into a near panic. But it was becoming obvious that Arthur sensed he was in the way, and in an effort to resolve the hospital's problem he asked me if I could let him have a small piece of land on which to put a caravan. He said that he had just enough money to buy one and that, once on his feet, he was sure he could manage. His words did not carry much conviction, but I felt so ill at ease at having to keep up a continual pretence that, after much thought, I finally decided I must tell him the truth.

There is no denying that it cost me a great effort, and I had to wait until I felt I had steeled myself sufficiently to be able to break the news gently and kindly. Once I embarked I found that it was not as difficult as I had feared, and to my astonishment I saw a look of relief spread over his face. He relaxed against his pillow and said, 'Thank you, Len, for letting me know. It's not knowing that is the worst of all.'

From that moment I felt a bond between us, and it was inconceivable that I should say that I had failed to find an alternative place for him, and then just walk away. One day when I found him looking especially despondent, the idea came to me of inviting him back to the now empty Le Court. I don't think it really occurred to me that he would accept, for the house now contained scarcely any amenities and he knew there would be nobody to nurse or even cook for him. But at least, I felt, it was a gesture. To my great surprise he seized on the offer almost before it was out of my mouth and then said, 'I'd love to come, Len.'

Although I was saddled with an unlooked-for encumbrance, I think that I was subconsciously pleased at having a problem to get my teeth into. I was immediately confronted by the dilemma of the nursing. With a volume of debts still to pay, I had no means of employing a nurse, neither could I see any hope of finding one who would work voluntarily. I was

irritated by the matron for having landed me with a problem
which I felt belonged to the National Health Service, and
equally irritated by the Health Service itself, and the many
other organizations I had approached, for not offering any
help. Being resentful is perhaps as good a stimulus as any for
proving that you can do what neither you nor anyone else
thinks you can, and, with only four days to prepare for
Arthur's arrival, I explained my predicament to a local nurse I
knew. She said quite simply, 'I don't think that's much of a
problem. I'll show you what to do and you do it, until we can
work out a better arrangement.'

Nothing worked out as I imagined it would. In hospital I
had only known Arthur sitting up in bed, and so I naturally
concluded that, once installed in Le Court, there he would
remain, a docile and grateful patient. But no sooner was he
out of the vehicle in which the hospital had sent him, than we
started a fight. He was now much thinner than in his pig-
keeping days a few months earlier, so I didn't anticipate much
difficulty in carrying him up the back stairs, even though they
were quite long and steep. But Arthur was having nothing to
do with that. He refused to be lifted, and he behaved in such a
way that in the end I was forced to give up, even though he
could not stand, let alone walk, without support.

Painfully we made our way upstairs in a kind of tandem
formation, stopping every three steps or so to draw breath.
Had he been reasonable, he would have been comfortably
settled in bed in a fraction of the time it eventually took. I
firmly resolved to win the next battle. I am not sure that I
won any of the battles, not even the very last. Arthur had
made what amounted to a declaration of independence the
moment he entered the front door. He looked for all the
world like a man who had been a long time in the wilderness

and now, at last, was in his own home and quite clearly intended to make the most of it.

For myself, I suppose that I did not mind too much, once I had come to terms with it, for there was enough on my mind not to want to fight any unnecessary battles. My own future was still in the melting pot. I was anxious to get on with my real vocation in life, if only I could discover what it was. But I had to deal with the debts and the infuriatingly complex formalities of selling a mortgaged estate piecemeal. It was summer, the only lawnmower was past its best, and the two acres or so of lawn – there had once been eight gardeners to tend the gardens – were growing fast. I knew that if the grass grew longer than the blades of the mower could cope with, I would be sunk, and so whenever I could get out of the house I attacked those lawns as if they were an enemy struggling to get the better of me. But it kept me fit and, I think, gave me the kind of safety valve that I needed.

I had all but wiped out the losses left by the community and was beginning to look ahead to the day when Le Court would finally be sold and I would be free to take up a new life. But what kind of life? Not in business, not in any of the professions, not in politics, just something that carried on where the war had left off. A world that would no longer resort to mass violence and be at the mercy of the next aggressor; a world free from confrontation and divisions: that was about the closest I came to defining my future hopes.

By early August, nearly three months after Arthur had arrived at the empty Le Court and accepted such care as I was able to give him, I could see that his end was not very far off. One evening when I was sitting by his bed before wishing him goodnight, he looked at me closely and said:

'You're thinking of selling Le Court, aren't you, Len?'

'Yes,' I replied. 'Sooner or later I shall have to decide on my career, and whatever it turns out to be I can hardly go on living here by myself in a twenty-five-bedroomed house.'

This was such an obvious conclusion that I wondered why he had asked the question. But his eyes, I noticed, were still thoughtful and he seemed to be searching for the right words.

'Well, I think you're wrong, Len. I can't bring myself to believe that all this has happened just for me, and I feel there must be something else behind it. I think you'll find that there are others like myself who haven't anywhere to go. I'm not suggesting that you go out and look for them. I'm just saying that if somebody else comes along, whoever it might be, don't turn him away. Please take him in, and please don't sell this house.'

The way Arthur spoke, so quietly and with an air of such assurance, surprised me. But looking after an old man in the final weeks of his life, or twenty old men for that matter, bore no relation to the direction I thought that I wanted my life to take. I was totally unequipped, let alone qualified, to do that kind of work. If any other counter-argument were needed, the National Health Service had been designed to cover just this kind of need. True, at the early stages there might be the odd exception – the person who for one reason or another was unlucky enough not to find a bed – but given a year or two this shortcoming would be made good. Because of the bond that had developed between us and the respect in which I held Arthur's opinions, I concealed my doubts and began speculating with him on how one might set about establishing such a home if ever the occasion should arise.

But here, too, I was proved wrong. It came to pass exactly as Arthur had foreseen.

Once again it was the telephone that set everything in motion. This time it was the porter of a block of flats in which one of my aunts lived. Aunt Edith, who had always had a strong sense of duty, felt that I was wasting my time at Le Court and not responding to the challenge of the post-war world as I should, and she had evidently conveyed something of her feelings to the porter.

After a brief word of introduction he began to tell me about his grandmother-in-law, a lady of ninety-one, who was living alone in a fifth-storey flat, unable to get out of bed and with only the district nurse to look after her. Finally he came to the point. Would I take her? I don't quite know to this day how it happened, but with hardly a thought as to the implications of what I was doing, I heard myself saying that I gladly would. Only then did I remember that there were no sheets, blankets or even mattresses left in the house. All of them had been sold to help pay off the debts. By the middle of the morning, however, I had managed to borrow the essentials from local friends, and the room was just about ready when Granny, as I came to know her, arrived in a very smart London County Council ambulance. The ambulance men carried her out on a stretcher, fully dressed and wearing a most remarkable hat crowned with a pheasant's tail feather which waved up and down in time to the men's steps.

As the small procession made its way into the house, up the stairs and finally to the room that I had hastily prepared, the drivers, I noticed, looked mildly surprised at the bare walls and sparse furnishings. They managed not to voice their feelings and, having gently deposited the old lady on the bed, politely thanked me and left.

The third person to come was Alf Wilmot, an upholsterer

from Hackney, a cockney through and through, whose good humour and ready wit were to become a feature of life at Le Court, but whose persistent dry cough betrayed even to my untrained ears the symptoms of advanced tuberculosis. The others who followed came from different social back-grounds and were in varying degrees of need. By the summer of 1949 the house had twenty-four residents.

One particular problem during this period was deciding how best to allocate the rooms so as to suit individual needs and make for minimum effort. Initially I had put Arthur in the former butler's room at the top of the back stairs, with the kitchen and office underneath and an adjacent bedroom for myself. When Granny came, Arthur and I had to move to the opposite side of the house, where the main bedrooms had been and which commanded a magnificent view across the garden to the distant Sussex downs. I had to put the tuberculosis patients downstairs, in the large drawing-room – or perhaps it had been the ballroom – where they could be isolated from the others. I moved my own room periodically in order to be close to whoever was most in need of attention at night.

Some of the residents were bedridden, some were in wheelchairs, some were able to walk with a little help, and one or two were physically fit but for one reason or another unable to manage on their own at home. The fact that Arthur and Granny had been obliged to make arrangements for their National Insurance to be brought to them at Le Court had made our activities known in official circles, and it was from the Hackney Assistance Officer that Alf Wilmot came to us. This, in turn, led to an enquiry from the tuberculosis wing of a London hospital as to whether we could help by taking some of their patients, who, it was said, no longer needed treatment and were, therefore, using urgently needed beds. For each one we accepted we received £5 a week – an enormous boost to our finances. Others came from the surrounding towns and villages. Never in my life would I have imagined that the pleasant Hampshire countryside could have hidden so many people living on their own and dependent upon the help of neighbours to cope with the everyday tasks of life.

Arthur died towards the end of August 1948. Although I had not realized it when he came to Le Court, he was a Roman Catholic who had long since given up his faith. During his three months with us he had steadily regained it, acquiring in the process a serenity and a sense of purpose that made him an altogether different person from the one I had originally known. It was through him that I first heard the Catholic Church's teaching and faith, and as a result eventually became a Roman Catholic myself. There was no greater gift that Arthur could possibly have given me.

As the household grew and news of what was happening spread, helpers began to appear. A few came through local contacts and friends, a few as a result of their association with the original community scheme, and one, in a way I have never fathomed, arrived from Paris. He was unusually strong and active and stayed for nearly six months, and I don't know how we would have managed without him. Another person who dramatically changed the scene was Frances Jeram, a hospital almoner from Portsmouth, who first came to help in her free evenings and finally gave up her job to settle in full time, for just pocket money.

Nursing presented us with the greatest difficulty of all. A year after the arrival of Arthur we still had no trained nurse, despite the fact that, in addition to routine day and night attendance, we were faced with the care and treatment of bed sores, with coping as best we could with one rather unpleasant external carcinoma and, worst of all, with the disposal of sputum from the tuberculosis ward without any proper facilities. For as long as it had been just Arthur and myself in the house, life had not really been too difficult. True, there was a great deal that needed to be done, for Arthur's cancer had spread to the liver, with the result that he gradually lost control of his bowels and could need emergency washing at any time of the day or night. But in a sense there was nothing serious at stake, for no treatment on earth could save his life, or even prolong it, and if things were not done exactly as they should be Arthur did not really mind. If anything, it seemed to cement our relationship rather than the reverse: I can still recall him saying, when I was being particularly clumsy, 'Makes us both feel rather humble, doesn't it?'

But now with a household of nearly thirty people, with such a wide range of disabilities and diseases, it was somewhat different. It was not surprising under these circumstances that the local GP and a number of other people expressed their misgivings about the project, arguing that this was not the kind of responsibility that a layman should undertake. Suppose, they asked, one of the patients came to harm through not receiving the right attention? I could only answer that I had never for a moment dreamed of becoming involved in work such as this; that far from looking for it, I had done everything in my power to find someone else to offer the shelter and care that were needed, and that, however unsatisfactory from a medical point of view Le Court might be, the alternative for every single person who had been accepted was considerably worse.

The tuberculosis cases had all been referred by hospitals, in several cases accompanied by a doctor's certificate stating that all the patient needed was a month's convalescence. In fact many of these turned out to be terminal cases who only lived for a few weeks and were highly infectious. The doctors in question were in the same situation as Arthur Dykes's matron found herself. The waiting lists for available beds in their hospitals were so long and the needs so urgent, that almost at any cost a patient who could no longer benefit from treatment had to be moved elsewhere. If news were received of a 'home' that could offer a bed, the doctor understandably assumed that it conformed to accepted nursing standards.

But there was a still more fundamental objection, which, to my surprise, came from a number of directions. 'If you feel that you *have* to devote yourself to this kind of work,' people said, 'don't you think that it would be more productive to concentrate on those who have a chance of getting better? Then you will have given them back an active life.'

The fact that such a question could be asked at all was symptomatic of the prevailing attitude towards the long-term disabled. In both the public and the official minds, they were placed at the very bottom of the list of medical priorities. Here again I could only answer that I had never for one moment contemplated becoming involved in this kind of problem. I had done so because without any prompting of my own I had unexpectedly been confronted with a handful of men and women, for none of whom any alternative source of help could be found. Did it really make sense to turn my back on them and set off in search of others who, though conceivably in greater need, might require help of a kind that I was not equipped to give?

In any case, if, as I understood them to be saying, the

correct course of action when you want to help your fellow man is to determine the area of greatest human need, who on earth is competent to define that specific area?

In my view the only question that matters is not whether one category of need is greater than another, but whether this is *my* niche, whether this is the field in which *I* am being called to work. Nevertheless, the significance of this particular line of reasoning has left its mark on me and I suspect it was one of the factors, even at that very early stage, which made me come to look upon my involvement with disabled people as a major challenge, not just a temporary diversion.

In the meantime, there were a number of harsh realities to face. With hospital almoners asking us to take some of their patients, in addition to the tuberculosis cases, we were beginning to receive more maintenance grants, although they were still small. We were not yet a registered charity – and therefore could not appeal for public funds – and we never quite knew from week to week how we were going to pay the bills. The house was in a bad state of repair; the electricity plant, installed just before the turn of the century, had broken down beyond repair and the long, steep drive had so many potholes that visitors and helpers were reluctant to commit their cars to it more often than they had to. Worse still, the household lacked any proper organization or control and, so far as I could see, would never gain it until we could find an experienced nurse to take charge. I can still vividly recall the acute sense of frustration and helplessness at knowing that a system and a routine were urgently needed, but having no idea how to set about providing it. Yet, on looking back to those confused and hectic days, I think that probably all this was actually a blessing. Being thrown together as we were at Le Court, and faced with possible collapse if we did not each contribute whatever we could, we acquired a kind of togetherness, and discovered in ourselves certain strengths and abilities which we had not known we possessed.

To call ourselves a family would perhaps be presumptuous: no disparate group, however close it may become, can really take the place of a natural family. But we felt our dependence on one another. If there were a decision to be taken that affected the household, then all those who were capable of making a constructive contribution were consulted. Practically all the residents helped in some way with the household chores. Trimming and filling the lamps was a regular daily task that occupied three people. Even old Granny, who never failed to remind me of the fact that seventy years ago she had been a district nurse, and who could be totally deaf, partially deaf or not deaf at all according to how it suited her, had a daily bucket of potatoes brought up to her room to peel. If she chose not to peel them, then they were cooked in their jackets, which she strongly disliked. So, in the end, she peeled them. That was one of my small victories.

Whether in all cases this policy were medically sound I do not know; in some instances probably not. But what I do know is that many who arrived in a state of acute apathy, hardly caring where they were put or what they were given to eat, soon began to take on a new lease of life. Whether they had come from their own homes, where the majority had been living alone and in steadily deteriorating conditions, or from hospital, where most must have realized they were just blocking a badly needed bed, few could see any purpose or point to their lives. Now, suddenly, they found that they were needed and that there was something useful and necessary for them to do. In consequence, I think it is true to say that, despite all that was lacking in terms of organization and material comforts, the household had a sense of purpose, a vitality, and generally speaking was a happy community.

Had it been otherwise, and had we had the money to buy everything we felt we needed, the whole future would almost certainly have been very different. To begin with, I would inevitably have imposed my own preconceived ideas on the way the household was structured and managed, and we would have conformed far more to the pattern of a traditional nursing home than what we so obviously were: a struggling, pioneering venture.

As it was, and without at the time realizing it, I was being given a most valuable practical lesson in the fundamental human needs and desires of the disabled person. I was being shown in an unforgettable way their basic longing, not to be treated as if they were helpless and waiting to have everything done for them, but, on the contrary, longing to be up and doing it themselves, to the very best of their ability. They wanted to feel useful and needed, to find a purpose and a challenge to their lives, to have sufficient independence and opportunity to lead a life of their own choosing. Above all, I found they wanted to be givers to society, not just receivers.

Chapter Two

ONE SMALL STEP

The late summer of 1949, just twelve months after Arthur Dykes's death, brought a climax in the affairs of Le Court. It was now evident that there was a continuing need for the services it was offering, at least into the foreseeable future, and it was imperative that some action be taken to bring the Home and its finances under proper control. I took the only step that seemed open to me – a traditionally British one in the face of an impasse – and formed a committee, in the hope that it would gradually assume overall responsibility for running and maintaining the Home.

After what I can only describe as a tumultuous beginning, dominated by the almost unanimous view that nursing homes cannot be run without adequate money and that the only really responsible step was to close the Home, organize a large appeal and then make a fresh start on a proper footing, the committee gradually settled into its stride. I think that the authorities would have carried out their threat to close us down had anyone been able to suggest where to send the twenty-four residents. Moreover, money or no money, the Home continued to function. To give the exchequer a boost, a garden fête was hurriedly organized, opened by Eamonn

Andrews. Suddenly Le Court emerged from obscurity to become a small part of the local scene.

Apart from the shortage of money, the main task facing the committee was revision of the admissions policy. The household at that time consisted not only of men and women of widely varying age groups and forms of disability, but there were also a number of TB patients. These, it was soon agreed with regret, would have to be phased out as quickly as possible, for even though physically separated from the others, they nonetheless constituted a health risk. In addition, their condition required that they should be in a home or unit specially equipped to give them the care that they needed. For me, it was a particularly sad moment, for I had come to feel a special affinity with these men and women, some still relatively young, who had come to live with us for what remained of their days. But the argument for moving them was irrefutable, and it may well be that I should never have accepted them in the first place.

Amongst those who remained there was one who stood in a completely different category from the others, and whose presence amongst us was to affect the future of Le Court and all the other Homes that were to follow.

Johnny Moore was sixteen, fair-haired and blue-eyed, bursting with vitality and self-confidence, over-confident at times, but never in a way that offended. Just after his fourteenth birthday he had contracted a rare disease, transverse myoletis, which apparently was rife in the early part of 1947 in the south of England.

The evening before he became ill, he had gone to the local cinema, and suddenly found that his feet were tingling, rather, he describes, as they feel when one has jumped from a high wall on to a pavement. The following morning he woke up completely numb from the waist down. Not surprisingly, his family was thoroughly alarmed, but the only medical advice he could get was that there was nothing to worry about and that he should be all right the following day. By an incredible piece of good fortune an Australian doctor called on the family that afternoon in search of a house to buy. He looked at Johnny, realized that he was urgently in need of catheterization, and told his father to get him into hospital at once or he would not be alive by evening.

The hospital to which Johnny was taken had done everything in their power, but it had not been possible to arrest the spread of the disease, and finally Johnny became completely paralysed from the waist down. At first he was placed in the medical ward, amongst patients older than himself and suffering from a wide variety of illnesses. He was happy enough, except for the fact that a lot of people seemed to die there; in fact eighteen in sixteen days, one in the very next bed. This, in his own words, 'so put the wind up' him that he was moved to the orthopaedic ward where there were many young people, and of course, many accident cases. There he remained for two years, until he was transferred to us at Le Court.

It was the first time in my life that I had come face to face with a young person, mentally alert and in full possession of all his senses, yet who was almost totally dependent upon other people for many of his daily living needs. His lower limbs were locked in a knees-up position with his feet more or less intertwined, and his thigh and calf muscles wasted. His arms, however, were strong and supple so that, once he had jiggled his wheelchair into the correct position, he could lift himself into bed and back again.

We soon learned to provide handlebars fixed at appropriate heights to give him access to the toilet without help, and to make manoeuvring in bed more simple, and I watched with interest and admiration the way he did everything in his power to manage on his own.

Johnny's bedroom was on the first floor, and three or four times a day I would carry him up and down the stairs, an exercise which I used to enjoy, but he, I suspected, did not, for the reason that he thought he was being a nuisance. We were extremely short-handed at the time and often Johnny would have to wait in his wheelchair at the top of the stairs until I was free to come and get him. This used to make him impatient, so much so that on one occasion he attempted the stairs on his own. The staircase was old-fashioned with very broad oak steps and a small landing in the middle. He managed to bump down the first flight of eight steps without losing his balance, but the right-angled turn of the landing proved too much for him, and he ended up on the floor with the wheelchair on top of him. Fortunately, neither he nor the chair were apparently any worse for the venture.

Although having to be carried up and down the stairs was a trial for Johnny, it served to bring us closer together, and helped me to understand something of what it meant to be still in one's teens and physically disabled. Until then I had hardly given the matter a moment's thought, and now that I began to reflect I found it extraordinary that a boy of his age seemed to be able to adjust so easily to such a traumatic experience, and I felt that I must know more.

In answer to my questions, Johnny said that he had been brought up to make the most of whatever came along, and that it was in his nature to come out on top if he possibly could. In hospital he had learnt to sit back and think out just where he really stood, and this had helped him to adapt to what he could see was inescapable. He kept repeating, 'You've got to think and meditate about it all otherwise you'll never adapt, and if you don't manage to adapt you're sunk.' He also said that rather than walk clumsily and slowly, which was the best he could do when he was first allowed out of bed, he had opted straightaway for a wheelchair, and this had given him a psychological advantage as well as much more mobility.

There was probably much more I could have learned from Johnny, but the affairs of Le Court were forcing me to consider very carefully the direction that the Home was to take. In particular, it was being impressed on me by the committee that we could not go on caring for such a wide variety of human needs under one roof and still give to each person the personal attention and quality of life that he or she needed. In addition, we were being petitioned very strongly to give priority to young disabled people, like Johnny Moore. This plea came principally from Miss Cherry Morris, the 'queen' of hospital almoners, who had been one of our first visitors from the professional world, and who, by her standing and experience, seemed to set the seal of official approval on what we were doing.

Her contention was that up and down the country, hidden away in hospital 'chronic wards' – wards for the very old and often senile – were large numbers of young, mentally alert disabled people, eking out a dreadful existence. There was no greater service we could render with the facilities at our disposal, she said, than to direct our attention to them. So long as we made sure that the majority were young, and that emphasis was given to creating a youthful atmosphere, there would be no objection to including a proportion of older residents. Indeed just as in a natural family the grandfather, or grandmother, often remain in the house without in any way dampening the life and vitality of the young, but rather adding to its happiness by virtue of their experience and dignity, so it could be with us. If, on the other hand, the majority were old, we could not admit a few of the young. The young person does not fit into an old people's environment.

No one on the committee had a serious counter-proposal to put forward, and even if they had, I doubt whether we would have been swayed by it. What Cherry Morris had portrayed so effectively in words, Johnny had driven home in his own way by his presence. We all felt that we had stumbled upon an area of need that had been hitherto overlooked.

At this point, early in 1950, the likely future course of events was beginning to become clearer. The committee was finding its feet; Le Court was settling down to a more orderly routine; helpers and financial support were being mobilized; and the new policy of admitting the younger physically disabled was being steadily implemented. The National Health Service was forging ahead and clearly regarded itself as the body that would provide all our medical needs, from the cradle to the grave. No one believed that there would be further need for homes like Le Court.

My own role, it seemed clear, was diminishing. I could not hand over the running of the Home to the committee and still continue to live in the Home; neither could I cut myself off completely, at least for the time being. In a way I was back where I had started at the end of the war, still convinced that there was something special that I wanted to do, but not knowing what it was or where to find it.

Then, quite unexpectedly, at the suggestion of Air Chief

Marshal Sir Ralph Cochrane, my former wartime AOC, I was offered a job on Barnes Wallis's swing-wing aircraft project, which after a good deal of wavering I accepted. It was a curious kind of decision, one that was a far cry from the kind of career that had so dominated my thoughts at the end of the war. But because I was still confused, I needed something concrete to do, and I felt that perhaps the moment was ripe to move away and look at life from a new perspective. Added to this was the fact that I had the highest regard for Barnes Wallis whose marvellous invention had inspired the Dam Busters, and I possibly felt too flattered to do anything but accept the offer.

For a while everything went smoothly enough. Le Court was settling down to its new routine, and I was spending the week days at Predannack (a former RAF aerodrome near the Lizard in Cornwall where the swing-wing field trials were being conducted in secret), and the weekends at Le Court. Then, rather suddenly, everything began to come apart. Contrary to expectations, Le Court was besieged with more applications for admission than it could possibly accept, mostly from the young disabled. One applicant, an ex-frogman who was being evicted from one boarding house after another because he was an epileptic, and whom Le Court turned down for fear of injury to the other residents, wrote directly to me. The letter was so worded as to make it virtually impossible to turn my back on his case, and I invited him down to spend a month's holiday in the cottage in which I was living at Mullion, near Predannack.

The result was the starting of a new Home, St Teresa's. From the moment the news of its founding began to filter through the local community, it uncovered the same kind of need as had been revealed at Le Court in its early days. This time, however, I co-opted almost from the very beginning the help of a small local committee, a step which was to prove decisive.

The Home, if one can use such a euphemistic term for what it was in those early days, was situated in the former station HQ of RAF Predannack. The building had been empty and neglected for some five years, its metal window frames long since rusted by salt-laden gale-force winds which blow during the winter months, and at one stage cows had broken in and made the building their temporary abode. There was no mains electricity, no sewage facilities, and no water nearer than a farmer's tap a hundred yards or so away. In return for a promise to vacate at a month's notice, the Air Ministry gave permission for its use, and barely three months after we had started work on the buildings, the first residents arrived. Within nine months the Home was full, and applications were still coming in.

I knew then that there was still a full-time job for me amongst the disabled people, and with a mixture of regret and embarrassment I asked Barnes Wallis if he would release me from the swing-wing project. Just as I was on the point of starting a third Home a mile or so from St Teresa's, I was diagnosed as suffering from TB in the left lung and was taken to the sanatorium in Midhurst where I remained for the next two and a half years under the expert care of the Australian lung specialist Sir Geoffrey Todd.

My enforced retirement from the active scene of operations was to bring about a profound change in the organization of the Homes. My father had bought two cottages on the Le Court estate, converted them into a house, and moved there with Mother to be on hand if I needed him. He now persuaded me that the most important step at this stage was to put everything on a proper legal footing by creating a charitable foundation. This would be composed of a central body of trustees and would act as the source of authority in law for the activities of the existing two Homes and any others that might be established.

One might suppose that I would have had little difficulty in agreeing to such an obvious and logical proposal. But the problem was that to do so involved relinquishing the personal control that I had hitherto exercised and handing it over to the trustees. I found it extraordinarily hard to take this step. Indeed, had it not been for the fact that I was immobilized in bed, with a good deal of surgery ahead of me and no certainty of when I would be free to leave the sanatorium, I do not believe I would ever have taken it. Yet it was possibly the most crucial decision I was ever to take in respect of the Homes, without which their accelerating expansion would never have been possible.

As I look back on those early years, which set the pattern for the future, I can now see just how providential was that period of hospitalization in King Edward VII Sanatorium. The enforced handing over of control of the Homes to the trustees proved to have a liberating rather than a restrictive effect. Inevitably, the new arrangement would need time to settle down. Like the original committee at Le Court, the newly formed trust under the chairmanship of Sir Arthur Denning (later to become Lord Denning) was startled at the disparity between the available funds and the cost of running Le Court and St Teresa's, both of which were in such a poor structural state that they would soon have to be rebuilt.

To add a further complication, the drawing up of the constitution and selection of the trustees had taken longer than expected and during this period two further Homes opened – St Cecilia's in Bromley and St Bridget's at East Preston in Sussex. It was an unusual kind of arrangement with the reins held jointly by the recently formed committees on the spot and myself in my hospital bed. But we eventually came to terms with each other, and despite a few upsets, both Homes started to function in a reasonably short time. In addition, the exercise proved another stage in my schooling into the art of delegation.

In no way do I claim to be proficient in this skill. But I do think that I have learned how essential it is for any undertaking that wants on the one hand to expand and on the other to remain personalized and human at every level of its operation. When I handed over control of the Homes to the trustees, I did so out of sheer necessity in the knowledge that this was the only way of keeping the Homes going. If I thought at all about my future role, I could only suppose that it would have to be a much restricted one, depending upon the extent to which I could persuade the trustees to embark upon any new venture. The committees would feel liberated from their sense of someone looking over their shoulder to see how they were getting on and, in consequence, would regard the Homes as their own personal responsibility. The fact that they were now answerable to a body of trustees, all of whom were distinguished in their particular field, gave a stature and credibility to the Foundation that it could never otherwise have had.

From my own point of view, having relinquished the reins gave me a number of advantages that I had not foreseen. My relationship with the individual committees became healthier and more constructive, and I could maintain personal contact without causing them to wonder whether I would intervene in their management, while still be available to attend a function or share a problem or speak up on their behalf.

In December 1954, when I was finally discharged from the sanatorium, though with stringent conditions as to how much work and travelling I could do, I attended my first trustees' meeting to discuss the immediate future. Circumstances were very different from two and a half years ago when I had left Vickers Armstrong to devote myself fully to the Homes. I was now overwhelmed by the urgency of providing more beds. Cherry Morris's conviction that up and down the country hundreds of mentally alert young disabled people were languishing in old people's wards had been abundantly proved, and from all sides we received requests for help. Faced with this, the trustees approved the suggestion that, while they concentrated on working out how the Central Foundation could best fulfil its role, I could do my best to establish two further Homes – but only two.

The Homes in question were both Historic Buildings, Ampthill Park House in Bedfordshire and Staunton Harold in Derbyshire. Both were large, Staunton particularly, and in a state of extreme dilapidation having been empty since the end of the war. In each case, the trustees gave me a free hand to act on their behalf, so long as I made certain that a local committee was put firmly in charge from the very beginning. I moved in, first to Ampthill and then on to Staunton Harold, to help make the two buildings habitable and to raise local support.

They were happy days for me, a release from the physical confinement of hospital, and a return to the work of converting an empty and discarded house into a home for those whose lives had lost purpose and meaning. The challenge of Staunton, in particular, was an experience I can never forget. Within an ace of being torn down by a speculator at the time we acquired it, after having stood for 500 years as the family seat of the Earl Ferrers and the pride of the district, it suddenly became the focus of the local community's interest.

The Ministry of Works wanted the building preserved but they had not succeeded in finding a buyer. Now that we had stepped in they could scarcely have been less cooperative. They had estimated that the repairs would cost £130,000 and stated that since work of this magnitude could not possibly be undertaken by volunteers with no money at their disposal they would not give our application their backing. But they were soon proved wrong. Indeed, their very attitude goaded the local people, who organized themselves into teams, each of which was allocated a specific room or part of the building to repair and renovate. At weekends it was a common sight to see fifty or more volunteers turn up with tools and materials, and without any prompting or fuss set about their respective tasks.

When the men had completed the structural repairs, the plastering and finally the painting, the women would arrive with curtains, chair-covers and so on. As soon as one room was ready, in came the first residents who participated as best they could, and thereby gave to the whole undertaking a new purpose and sense of urgency. A young reporter who came up to see what was happening found the Dowager Lady Ferrers bearing down on him with a broom. 'Young man,' she said, 'take this and go and sweep out the kitchen. You'll find it at the end of that corridor. A very large room. Off you go.' And off he went.

One memorable day, during a national strike, a local quarry came to re-macadam our long and unserviceable drive. The owners donated the tarmac – ninety tons of it – and the men gave their time, some of them leaving home at three in the morning in order to have the tarmac heated and ready for the first shift of lorries. Who could forget such occasions as those?

Staunton Harold, however, was to prove the completion of the first stage in the development of our Homes in the United Kingdom, and for me personally a preparation for a new life involving work overseas as well as at home. Attitudes towards disabled people were now changing, both among the public and in government and local authority circles. The licensing of Homes such as ours was no longer quite so easy as it had been, for required standards of building and associated facilities were steadily rising, though to counterbalance this, weekly maintenance grants for residents were becoming more available from the local authorities.

This meant that more money was available for modernizing our old houses to make them more suitable for disabled people. Le Court and St Teresa's had already replaced their crumbling buildings with purpose-built new ones, and the day was approaching when a committee would inaugurate a different way of operating by beginning with a new, specially designed Home. I sensed the first signs of change, and my thoughts were increasingly turning towards new tasks outside Britain.

The sequence of events that was to take me abroad, started with a letter that I received in 1953 while still in the sanatorium. It was from a Scotsman living in the Nilgiri Hills of South India who said that he had a great desire to do something for the disabled and destitute, but that as he was neither a doctor nor a missionary, he could not find any way of becoming involved. He had heard of the Homes in England and wondered whether there was any possibility of doing something similar in India.

To prove that he was more than a casual enquirer he flew to England to discuss his proposal, and offered his own house for use as a Home. It was difficult to see how I could respond in any practical way, but for what it was worth I promised that when I was out of hospital and fit enough to travel, I would come to India. Two years later, shortly after having moved into Staunton, I enlisted the help of two volunteer nurses, one of whom was returning to New Zealand, to go out as an advance party. On 1 December that same year, 1955, I went out myself and found a small out-patients clinic in operation. But whether the house could ever make a Home for disabled people I was unable to make up my mind.

Neither the six Homes that were then operating in Britain nor the central trustees thought very highly of this expansion to India. They argued that none of the Homes was financially secure; all were working to the limit to become so; and the extent of the need for further Homes was becoming more and more apparent. What possible good, they asked, could be served by abandoning the struggle here – battlefield seemed a more appropriate word at times – and taking on an even bigger challenge halfway across the world?

The same kind of argument had also been raised by Le Court when we started St Teresa's in Cornwall, but events had made it clear that while no one in Cornwall would for one moment have dreamed of supporting a Home in Hampshire, they would gladly throw themselves heart and soul into setting one up on their own doorstep. Could one therefore not assume the same reaction in the case of India? Could one not also argue that the very fact of being a broadly based venture in the process of expansion would attract more, rather than less, support? And, at the same time, would it not draw attention to the universal needs of disabled people? Nobody, I suspect, was convinced, but equally no one did more than try gently to dissuade me.

Almost everything that I was warned to expect in India turned out to be false. I was told, for instance, that the moment I started any kind of Home I would be flooded with people clamouring for a place, but if anything applications came in more slowly than in England, at any rate at the beginning. At Dehra Dun, where the Princess of Nabha offered us a large but dilapidated house, not a single applicant appeared for nearly six weeks after the house had been laboriously prepared. This nearly broke the hearts of the committee, who not unnaturally felt that I had co-opted their support under false pretences. The true reason for this apparent reluctance to apply for admission was that, to the Indian way of thinking, it is not the proper thing to send a member of one's family to an institution, no matter how great his or her need. However, once it could be shown that this was not an institution, but a Home in the real sense of the word – an extension of the family system we called it – the response changed.

I was also told that a Home such as I knew in England would never work in India because of the caste system, which would lead to divisions and to people of different castes refusing to eat together. But in more than twenty years we have never had such a problem. Only once did one man object to another's presence in the dining-room, and eventually we had to affirm our principle and ask the protester to leave. The common denominators of suffering and human need, I find, bring solidarity and mutual understanding, not just among those who suffer themselves but among those who come to their aid.

At a more mundane level, I had imagined that land in India could be bought for a song even in the neighbourhood of a major city. On this bright assumption I used such capital as I had to buy a Land-Rover and converted an old thirty-two-seater bus into living and office accommodation. Three volunteers were following me by sea, and we planned to acquire a suitable piece of land and, using the bus as a base, to build a Home around ourselves with whatever local materials were available. I was in for a rude shock. In the first place, even jungle land well outside Bombay cost a minimum of £1000 an acre, and secondly, we had made a mistake in our import documentation, with the result that Bombay Customs promptly impounded the two vehicles and demanded £1800 for their release. Since the costs we had already incurred had left me with little more than £100 on landing in India, and since I had only one contact in Bombay – Nina Carney, wife of the chief engineer of Burmah-Shell – it looked as if we might have to abandon the mission.

These twin shocks however, though unpleasant, were salutary. Overnight, we became three men and one woman in a great hurry, knowing that if we did not find what we were looking for very quickly – a piece of land without the requirement of any immediate down-payment – we were sunk. What I had already seen of the Scotsman's house in the Nilgiris, high up in the hills and useless to any plainsman, had convinced me that our only hope was to open on as broad a front as we could in the shortest possible time, in order to win credibility and to find the calibre of Indian we needed to form the Central Trust.

This newly acquired sense of urgency communicated itself to those we met. In an unexpected way, the fact that we had no capital and that at times we had to think twice before taking a bus, let alone a taxi, brought us more support and help than the most professionally planned publicity campaign could ever have done.

The help that we so badly needed was forthcoming, and we found what we were looking for, and much more besides. Within three weeks, in return for a promise to pay when we could, we were given an acre and a half of land. It was a mile from the nearest road, but pleasantly sited on a hill with a distant view of Bombay airport.

Almost simultaneously, a Burmah-Shell contractor, at the prompting of Jimmy Carney, Nina's husband, offered us a three-roomed asbestos hut that he no longer needed and erected it for us free of charge. Hardly had I moved in than an 'ambulance' arrived with an old man whom the driver said he had found on the street and who was suffering from advanced cancer. He was such a likeable and friendly person that we called him Pop.

From then on, everything just seemed to happen in the most unexpected ways and in many other parts of India. The problem of the vehicles locked up in Customs took me to Delhi where I met the Chief of the Air Staff, Subreto Mukerjee. He listened to my story, wrote to the Head of Customs demanding the release of the vehicles, was told that he could have them as soon as £2000 was paid, and promptly replied that the Air Force would pay. Customs were so taken aback by this that they waived all charges and immediately released both the Land-Rover and the bus. This had the added effect of completely altering our standing in the eyes of officialdom in Bombay, and led to the offer of a property for a Home in Delhi.

News of what we were doing began to spread. The Catholic Archbishops of Calcutta and Madras invited me to visit them and each in turn gave us a large house. From a remote town of South India the widow of a Tamil civil servant wrote offering her services, as did a senior Army officer in Babina. The former had never undertaken any public work of any kind – I don't think she had even used a telephone – and yet within eighteen months she had started our first Home for leprosy. The latter, General Virendra Singh, set about collecting funds and was later to take charge of the whole Indian operation. My part, in those early days, was to spend as much time as I could with each of the little groups, helping to raise public support and interest, sharing the task of organizing life within the Home, and searching for suitable buildings.

If India was a land overflowing with the poor and the deprived, it was also a land filled with a great awareness of its responsibilities towards them, and with a friendliness and a generosity of an astonishing depth. For me India was the school in which I learned many lessons about how to work in another people's country. I first discovered how utterly different, and yet how essentially the same, man is the world over; and how innumerable are the ways that he can take to reach the same human goal. I also began to learn how careful we must be to respect other people's ways of doing things and to stop thinking that ours are necessarily better. Yet how easily we fall into this error. How many intelligent and sincere people there still are in foreign lands, who persist in believing that the 'natives' cannot be trusted to get on with a job and do it properly, without realizing that it is this very attitude, this mistrust, that causes the other man to withhold his true abilities and cooperation. India made me feel at home and welcome, despite what must have appeared to its people a peculiar way of setting about the work we had come to do. In consequence I found it easy, even enjoyable, to adapt to ways that had not been mine.

India proved to be the gateway through which the concept of the Homes flowed to other countries. My cousin Pam Hickey, whom I had not seen since the early 1930s and who lived in Singapore, invited me for a short stay. I arrived in the middle of the 1956 riots, when for several days a total curfew on all vehicles was imposed. Pam, always strong-minded and persuasive, obtained a special dispensation, and organized a visit to RAF Changi with a small military escort. As a result of this we happened across an empty seaside building, formerly the Jungle Survival School. The Treasury in London rejected the Commander-in-Chief's request that we be allowed to acquire it at a concessional price, so the Singapore Government bought it and rented it to us at a dollar a year.

Wilfred Russell, an English businessman who had helped us in Bombay, was sent on a fact-finding mission to West Africa and asked whether we would like him to 'throw around the suggestion of a Home'. The Prime Minister of Sierra Leone offered his house in Bo, so we despatched Margot Mason (now Mrs Gibb), one of our three original volunteers in India, to follow up this unexpected opportunity, and gradually a new series of new Homes was founded, in West Africa, Morocco and Jordan.

At every stage the initiative came not from ourselves, but always from the locality itself. A person from another country might visit one of the Homes, or learn of their existence, and would then write asking for information as to how he or she should set about establishing one locally. Occasionally a retired person with knowledge of another country would offer to go there at his own expense and see what he could do.

If it became clear that there was a serious desire for a Home, even though the interested group might be very small, we would give all the help we could, initially by correspondence and later by sending someone either to advise or to become actively involved in mobilizing public support. If asked, we would send a trained nurse, experienced in working overseas, to move into the house which the local committee had acquired and take charge in the initial period of establishing it as a Home. This period has sometimes lasted two or three years, but it has been one of our basic principles to rely upon local staff, as well as on a committee composed mostly of people indigenous to the country concerned and representative of the community in which the Home is situated.

Since it is this local committee that from the very beginning has to undertake full responsibility for financing and administering the Home, we have always felt it to be absolutely essential that the decision to start must be taken by its members of their own free will and without any undue prompting from ourselves. I think I can truthfully say that we have never tried to apply any form of persuasion on a local group which, after expressing an interest, has had second thoughts about whether to continue.

If you go anywhere with a sizeable sum of money in your pocket and say to people that you would like to see a Home started and ask them to assist, there is little doubt that enough men and women will be found to join the venture. But once the money runs out or the Home falls upon difficult days, the local group will inevitably turn to you for help. If, however, you come with nothing, or virtually nothing, and say, 'Look, here is a need. Here is Michael, or Subash, or Ivy, unable to walk, left alone in the corner of a room all day until the family comes back from work. Don't you think we could do something about it?', the relationship is entirely different. If there is no response at all, then you have failed; but if there is an enthusiastic reaction and the people you have spoken to commit themselves to the challenge, then you can be certain that they will never let go. Such, at any rate, has been my experience.

What they are committing themselves to is not simply a good cause or project, but people with names and faces who are in urgent and obvious need of help. They also become closely identified with the Home that they are planning to build, so that its success is their success, and its failure their failure. It develops into a personal challenge, and because it is fundamentally their undertaking, not yours, they find themselves in honour bound to see it through to the end.

During the thirty years that this process of expansion has been taking place, there has never been a single committee that has capitulated, no matter how great the difficulties which confronted it. Even during the Nigerian civil war, in the battered enclave of what was then called Biafra, the two committees concerned never abandoned the disabled children under their care. Both those Homes were over-run and damaged by the fighting, but the staff evacuated the children, brought them back behind the firing line and housed them in whatever temporary accommodation they could find until

the end of hostilities. Today a new, large and well-designed
building is situated at Orlu, not very far from the tiny
improvised airstrip that constituted the only lifeline of the
besieged Biafran community during those difficult days. To
me it stands as a symbol of the innate generosity and the deep
concern for their fellow human beings that one finds in
people's hearts, no matter their race, colour or creed. Sadly,
these qualities often seem to appear only when we come face
to face with another person's need; when we can see his
suffering and identify him as a human individual, very much
like ourselves.

To some people, I realize, this policy of waiting for a
situation to develop rather than planning the future will
appear a haphazard and unbusinesslike way of operating, and
in other fields of endeavour I readily admit that it might be.
But in my own circumstances, it was the only path open to
me during the formative years, and now that I reflect upon it
I believe it to be the safest and surest way forward for anyone
who wishes to tread a similar path. The day may come when
the Foundation in Britain should in some fields undertake a
greater degree of planning in order to be ready in good time
for the specific needs of the future, but if so I hope we can do
so without abandoning our previous policy.

Reduced to its simplest form, my reasoning goes
something like this: if I am suddenly confronted by someone
who is indisputably in need of urgent help, my first duty is to
discover where he can best obtain the particular attention that
he needs. If that help cannot be obtained, either because it
does not exist or because it is impossible to persuade those
who could help to do so, then I must consider what else can
be done. If the only option left to me is to accept
responsibility for the person myself, then I have a duty to

respond, and within the limits imposed by my personal circumstances, make the best arrangements I can for that person's care.

If I use my faculties and my resources to their full potential, limited and faulty though these may be, I feel that I can expect that the Providence of God will make good whatever I cannot do myself. Yet I emphasize the absolute necessity of working as if everything depended upon yourself, for I hold no brief for the view that if only you have sufficient faith you can sit back and God will provide.

Because I know that my involvement with disabled people has not been a journey of my own prompting, I have consistently felt in the bottom of my heart, even when everything seemed against us, that help in some form would ultimately arrive, though possibly not until the eleventh hour. At the same time I have to admit that there have been moments when I have not applied the criteria I should, and have turned aside to embark upon a project entirely of my own choosing. In these circumstances I have ultimately become aware that my behaviour and my attitude have been different, that I was more than usually anxious, even desperate to keep the project from collapsing.

As the organization becomes established and begins to achieve some success, there is a great temptation to branch out into new fields. Other forms of need are discovered, perhaps mentally handicapped children, or adults, the old and infirm, or the terminally ill. People come forward with suggestions that one start a magazine, join forces with this, that, or the other movement – some unquestionably sound, some hare-brained. Sometimes considerable pressure will be exerted, and cogent arguments put forward. One has by now gained confidence, or more probably over-confidence, in overcoming obstacles, and it is precisely then that one needs to beware. One has to balance the necessity of meeting the needs of those who have no one else to whom to turn, with that of not being diverted from one's true objective.

This raises the crucial question as to how one distinguishes between what is a genuine call and one that is not. If you find yourself confronted by a genuine human need which is not being met by existing services, and feel prompted to give up your business or profession in order to devote yourself full-time to doing something about it, how do you decide? What help can you gain from the experience of others who have taken a similar step?

It would be convenient to be able to give a simple formula by which the issue could be put to the test, but that is not possible. A calling of this kind is very personal and whoever sets out to offer advice should do so with caution and sensitivity, recognizing that each case can only properly be judged on its own merits.

The one clear imperative is to try and keep a clear head, to be as objective and dispassionate as possible, and at all costs to suppress any possible self-interest or personal ambition. Even the thought: 'I am the one person equipped to deal with this problem', may be dangerous. Self-justification so often disguises personal ambition.

If it were just a question of serving on a committee, helping a fund-raising drive, or even donating enough money to build a whole Home, the fact that one is motivated by a desire to enhance one's social standing does not seem to me to matter in the least. Good has been done that might otherwise not have been done and it can often happen that a person who starts this way will gradually change. Some will become totally committed, concerned solely with the well-being of the Home, or whatever it may be, and provide an example to the rest of the community.

To become the founder of a project with the intention of remaining personally responsible for running it is another matter. Here there has to be a genuine and disinterested commitment, and a singleness of purpose which those who may wish to become involved can recognize, and which is strong enough to overcome the inevitable obstacles and set-backs. The person concerned must be dedicated, and convinced that what he is setting out to do is a personal vocation. His decision must be based on a good reason and on the right reason, one which he is prepared when necessary to disclose and defend. If he finds that there is any major element in his motivation that he wants to keep to himself there is danger ahead. All of us have the right to give money or render service to a good cause for the wrong reason, but we do not have the same right if we are its initiator and sponsor.

I am fully aware that most of our motives are mixed, and that to become introspective and scrupulous is not a healthy sign. People often do worry and even refrain from seeking help because they are suspicious of their motives. I respect people who act in this way, but I feel they are wrong, just as I do those who justify not saying a prayer or not going to church on the grounds that they are only doing so because they need something. What matters is that we do whatever good we can, and that we do pray and go to church. How many of mankind's great journeys have begun with just a small step? Only when it is a question of setting something in motion which will affect other people's lives and well-being, do we need to be rather more careful than usual.

It is true that an inner prompting of this kind may be recognizable as genuine only by the people concerned.

Others may consider it false and misguided; in that case, after having put the idea to the test of others' judgement, we must make our own decision. It may well prove a lonely path at the beginning, but those who know that it is their path will find strength and consolation from the fact that at least they are walking it rather than still trying to make up their mind. My own advice would be to give the prompting the benefit of the doubt and, provided one has weighed it all up with an open mind, to take the plunge. We live in an age where there is a premium on caution, on clinging to financial and material security. A spirit of adventure, of putting oneself and one's future second and the needs of the deprived first comes as a breath of fresh air.

The decision, in any case, may well be governed by the practicalities of the situation. Are there family or other personal commitments which would be put at risk? I do not believe that one has the right to devote one's time to helping other people and as a result to neglect one's children or spouse. Is there a reasonable hope of finding the resources that the project will require? Some people have sound and well thought-out ideas but appear to be floating them in the hope of attracting the necessary money. Others have ideas that appear less convincing on a first hearing but are clearly determined to put them into practice, money or no money. It is to the latter that I normally pay more attention, for I know that given the personal commitment, the rest will follow, assuming of course that the proposal is genuinely filling a need. As a general rule, those who are willing to start in a small way, in a rented building if they can't afford to buy one, and who make do are the ones who will succeed. So long as the idea remains just a proposal on paper, no matter how good it may be, people will hesitate to give. But once a start has been made and there is something to see, money will begin to come. Not all projects can be started this way, but far more can than we tend to believe.

Starting from small beginnings and building up as and when one can carries a positive value all of its own. Breaking new ground, particularly when it has to do with people and their emotional, as distinct from medical, needs, is a better way than planning the result in advance. No plan can ever hope to have foreseen all contingencies and needs. It will almost certainly need to be modified, as we are continually discovering after thirty years' experience. To start with just three or four people, even in less than satisfactory standards of accommodation, means that one can adapt as the situation develops. One can, as it were, mould the facilities to fit the living contours of the people who are using them. Others may disagree, for the structure of contemporary society, with its vast institutions of government, favours planning at all levels of the nation's life. But for me it is the only way. Everything that has started small seems to be expanding. The few things that started big have all vanished.

Chapter Three

EXCEPT A GRAIN

In 1957 an incident occurred which made me question our first principles about the policy of full delegation of all aspects of my activities. At that time the Indian Foundation had recently become legally registered as a charitable society, with five Homes in operation and a sixth about to start. This latest Home represented something of a departure for us in that the American Jesuits had offered us a thirty-acre estate just outside Jamshedpur, the steel town of Bihar, on condition that we use it for children. Hitherto, we had not really considered children as coming within our terms of reference, and I had done a good deal of heart-searching before deciding that we were justified in entering this new field. The idea had found favour with the local community and a good committee had been formed, some of whose members were British or American businessmen working in the steel complex. On the particular day that I am describing I was being driven from Calcutta to Jamshedpur to attend a somewhat crucial committee meeting, at which the future policy of the Indian Homes was to be decided.

My host was Larry Donnelly, a personal friend and managing trustee of the Indian Foundation, dynamic and compassionate, and the main force behind the Homes in Calcutta and the surrounding area. Normally one would travel to Jamshedpur by train, but on this occasion Larry had business at Durgapur, a steel town about halfway along our route, and for the three or four hours that he was occupied there he arranged that I should visit the steelworks' hospital.

I don't always feel quite at ease being conducted round a hospital by a doctor in a foreign country. Usually he has only been given the briefest explanation as to who I am and why I am visiting, and therefore not unnaturally assumes that I have at least some specialized knowledge. As a result I cannot avoid feeling that I am there under false pretences and, what is worse, that I am using up a man's time that can be ill afforded. However, in this instance, it was clear that the doctor had very quickly placed me in the right category, for he spoke about the human and social problems that the individual patients faced as a consequence of their hospitalization, and about the role that the hospital played in the local community. It was obvious that he was proud of the high standard of medical and nursing care in the hospital, and I warmed to him as we completed our tour. To me it was yet another example of the progress that India had made in so many different fields since gaining her independence just ten years previously. Meanwhile my thoughts kept returning to the all-important committee meeting at Jamshedpur that evening. Consequently, it was with some relief that I heard the doctor say that we were now coming to the last ward.

We had scarcely passed through the doorway when I was conscious of being stared at with unusual intensity by someone at the far end of the ward. The feeling persisted as we made our way along the beds, stopping every now and then to ask a question of one of the patients, or perhaps just to offer a word of encouragement. When we finally came to the last bed I saw a young, alert man of perhaps twenty whose eyes were fixed on mine with an expression which made me feel as if I were the bearer of news that he had eagerly been awaiting. How there could be anything that he wanted to say to me, a stranger of whom he could not possibly have supposed anything, except that I was involved in the business of manufacturing steel? But for the first few moments his intense expression absorbed me to the exclusion of whatever the doctor was saying. When I turned and asked who the boy was and what was the matter with him, I felt that for the first time since we had started our round the doctor was a little ill at ease. He explained that this was a particularly sad case, that the boy had had a serious accident in the steel mill which had resulted in paralysis from the waist down. Every possible remedial treatment had been given to him, to the extent of flying in a specialist from Calcutta, but there was nothing further that could be done to improve his condition.

The doctor paused at this point as if waiting for me to make some comment, but I had caught sight of a rubber tube at the side of the bed and connected to a small bottle on the floor. I realized that the boy was incontinent as well as paralysed and therefore wore a catheter, or something of the kind. In spite of the paralysis of his lower body, his arms and his shoulders looked so unusually strong and his face so youthful and intelligent, that I might have been looking at Johnny Moore who had so surprised me when I first met him at Le Court eight years before. Johnny had not come to Le Court simply in order to carve out for himself the best niche in which to live out his days amongst us; he had come as a young boy on the threshold of life, whose eyes were already beginning to look beyond the walls of the house into the world around him. Within a year of his arrival he had felt confident enough to spread his wings and fly away to build a nest of his own choosing, out in the world as just another member of society. The same could be so of the boy in front of me, given only a long enough period of time in a Home such as one of ours, to learn how to manage in a wheelchair and for arrangements to be made regarding his catheter. Like Johnny, he could go on to marry and do a normal job.

Quite how long my reflections had taken I do not know, but I became aware that nobody had said anything for a while and that the boy was still looking as if he expected me to speak to him. I turned to the doctor, who was now clearly on the defensive, and who said, 'We are having to discharge him tomorrow morning.' When I asked where to, he replied, 'Home. To his family.' Then, as an afterthought, 'The company is being very generous and giving him a pension so that he can pay somebody to look after him if his family can't manage.'

I felt that I was beginning to understand why it was that both the doctor and the boy were behaving in this rather unusual way, and I asked whether home meant somewhere in the town of Durgapur itself or in one of the villages. The doctor answered that it was outside the town in a fairly remote village. The hospital staff had done their best to instruct the family in how to change and sterilize the catheter, and they could only now hope and pray that the family would succeed in carrying out their instructions properly. With this the full implication of what the doctor had been saying suddenly burst on me. Already there were sounds of the pre-monsoon thunder in the air, and once the monsoon itself arrived there would be literally no hygiene at all in the village. Before I could stop myself, I exclaimed:

'But in a village like that, without a protected water supply, and with no one who can really know anything about how to keep his catheter sterilized, what chance has he got?'

No sooner had the words been uttered than I regretted them, for I knew there was nothing the doctor could do about it and from his expression it was obvious that I had greatly upset him. He asked if I would mind coming outside to finish the conversation, as there was something more that he wanted to say. Once outside, the doctor told me what had obviously been lying heavily in his heart. The management of the hospital, he said, had done everything in its power to find a place where the boy could live in hygienic conditions and at least have his tube removed regularly and properly cleaned. But such a place, it seemed, did not exist. Homes for the disabled were unknown, hospitals had no vacant beds, and few private families in India could be reasonably expected to take in a stranger such as this one and accept responsibility for him. Already the boy had been in the steelworks' hospital for three months longer than he should have been, in the hope that something would transpire, but now with the greatest reluctance orders had been given that he must be moved. There were too many cases waiting for urgent treatment. The doctor's distress and concern were plain and, taking me by the arm he said:

'You must not judge us too harshly. You in the West are so fortunate. I know this, because I did some of my training over there and know what was available in the UK even before the Health Service. But I'm not quite sure that you always appreciate just how fortunate you are.'

Now it was my turn to feel on the defensive. It was indeed true that most of us in Britain had no idea just how fortunate we were with our National Health Service, and indeed all the other social welfare facilities that existed. But despite all that, the National Health Service had not been able to do any more for Arthur Dykes than the Durgapur hospital could now do for this boy. Who was I to appear to be standing in judgement on India and to have unwittingly forced the doctor to apologize to me? I tried to explain that our hospital service had its shortcomings and went on to assure him that I understood only too well the dilemma in which he found himself. But I am not sure that my words carried much conviction. In my embarrassment I mumbled something about our own Foundation and its work, and added that I was on my way to our Home at Jamshedpur and that, although it was open only to children, I would speak to the committee and ask if they could offer a place to this boy, even if only temporarily. The doctor led me back into the ward and indicated to the boy, who again fixed his eyes on me, that there was just a possibility that I might be able to find a Home where he could stay for a little while. As the doctor spoke, the expression in the boy's eyes changed, in a way that I do not think I will ever forget.

The committee meeting at Jamshedpur that evening proved to be one of those occasions when everything seemed to go wrong. I was certain that the committee would only have to hear about the plight of the boy to agree at once to accepting him, and therefore the logical step seemed to be to settle this at the very beginning so as to leave the rest of the evening free for the main items on the agenda. Already I had made two major mistakes. In the first place I should have known that when an agenda has been drawn up and circulated, committees like to keep to it, particularly when they are composed mostly of businessmen. That I introduced a completely new and unexpected item right at the beginning, almost before the chairman had been able to complete his opening remarks, such was my eagerness, disturbed the relaxed and friendly atmosphere that had characterized the opening of the meeting.

In the second place, I should never have taken for granted the agreement of the committee, particularly when there was so much at stake, for the result was to give them the impression that it was more or less a *fait accompli* in my own mind which they were expected merely to approve. Misgivings and objections followed fast one upon another. First, there was the legal point that the Home had been accepted on the condition that it was used solely for children. Admittedly it was a technical point, but nevertheless one that would have to be thought out and discussed with the Jesuits. Secondly, I had made a major point about the need for sterile and hygienic conditions, but the Home had been unoccupied for three years and was in a bad state of repair; there was only a skeleton staff and, even though one of them was a nurse, this was hardly the place to bring a boy such as I had described. Thirdly, the committee had both a moral and a legal responsibility to maintain proper standards of care and would have to answer publicly in the event of any mishap.

Against this I could only answer that the doctor at the hospital had himself agreed that the boy had virtually no hope of surviving in his village, and that whatever the defects of this Home, the conditions and care that the boy would receive there were infinitely superior to the alternative. But it was obvious that the committee was becoming frustrated and unsettled; time was passing and they still had not started on the business for which they had assembled. When the chairman, summing up the feeling of the meeting, said that whilst everyone agreed that somewhere should be found for the boy, under the circumstances it was felt I should ask one of the other existing Homes which were more experienced and better equipped, the matter was settled.

At that time I think that I was more surprised than hurt or offended. It just seemed incomprehensible that a committee as well intentioned and understanding as this one should be unwilling, at very little extra trouble to themselves, to save the life of a boy who had suffered an accident of a kind that was liable to happen any day in their own steelworks at Jamshedpur. But when the dust had settled, I realized that the whole situation must have looked very different to them and that there were other more deep-rooted doubts in their minds, which they could not very well voice. For one thing, they had set themselves the task of providing what they hoped would become a first-class Home for mentally handicapped children, and this was going to stretch their personal and material resources to the limit. I, too, was an unknown quantity to them. What guarantee was there that if they accepted this case, I would not come before them in a month or two with another request of equal urgency? India, after all, was full of people who died through lack of drainage and protected water supplies, not to mention lack of access to proper medical attention. However much they regretted their inability to help the boy, and this undoubtedly they did, was it not more responsible, and in the long run more effective, to concentrate on one specific goal and make certain of achieving that properly?

There was, moreover, one further mistake that I had made in putting the case, one I fear I was to repeat more than once in later years. Committees, I was to learn, do not really like completely new projects being thrown at them without warning. If there is something new to suggest, particularly if it is radical, the ground needs to be well prepared. Not only should as much notice as possible be given that a new proposal is going to be raised, but one should at the very least put the matter to the chairman and ask how he thinks the matter should be handled. Should, for instance, a memorandum be drawn up and circulated to the trustees, however hurriedly? Or would it be better first to speak to the chairman of the relevant sub-committee? It can also be a mistake to put forward a case so strongly as to force the meeting to vote. Far better to leave room for someone to suggest a counter-proposal which, at the best, may prove an equally good way of achieving the same objective, and at worst may succeed in keeping the proposal still alive.

Whether a more considered approach would have altered this particular decision I do not know. I doubt it. With the advantages of hindsight, I think that the committee was probably right and acted in the best interests of the Home. Today, run by an Order of Spanish and Indian Sisters with admirable dedication and professionalism, it stands as one of the finest Homes for severely retarded children of its kind that I have seen anywhere in the world.

But despite doing everything that I possibly could I was unable to find a Home that would accept the boy. Bombay or Delhi probably would have done, given time and on the assumption that the problem of a thousand-mile journey could be overcome, but time was lacking. The one organization that really helped me was the leprosarium belonging to Mission to Lepers at Purulia which I had visited two or three months previously and which had made a great impression on me. One of their doctors, who was familiar with the local dialect and accustomed to visiting villages, offered to try and find the boy and see what assistance he could give. A week or two later, when he had managed to do so, he reported that the village was situated some four miles off the most rudimentary of roads, and that even his four-wheel drive jeep had had great difficulty in negotiating the terrain. In any case, he was extremely sorry to report that the boy had already died, from what he gathered must have been an infection of the urinary tract.

This news left me with a sense of failure. On the one hand it was an experience which served to reinforce the obvious truth that I must respect and uphold a committee's right to decide its own affairs, so long as these were not contrary to our established ideals and principles. With newly formed committees in particular, I was beginning to learn that it was necessary to establish mutual confidence, to leave each one to find its own level, secure in the knowledge that whatever they were taking on was within their resources, even though this might be less than one would have liked. Each individual Home might be small, but at least there would then be a stable base upon which to build and expand. On the other hand, when it was a case of a particularly urgent appeal for help, such as we had just witnessed, I did not feel that I could hide behind the fact that all admissions to the Homes could only be decided by the management committees themselves, and leave it at that. It was not that I questioned the judgement or goodwill of the committee, nor the system under which we operated. Rather, I felt, that in this instance the appeal had been directed personally at me, that something new was being asked of me. How, within the framework of the organization I had brought into being, could I exercise some measure of independent action with regard to someone in genuine and urgent need for whom no other place could be found?

The truth is that I was in that unhappy state of knowing that something had to be done, unable to identify what and where, and convinced that whatever it was must be done today and not put off until tomorrow. This is a phenomenon that I have noticed both in myself and in others: a genuine call to embark upon a new venture, or perhaps a new career, is preceded by an insistent sense that there is something that you are expected to do, that some change in life is to come about, and so the senses have become alerted. About its importance and its general direction you are absolutely certain, but as to the specifics – what, how or where? – you are lost. You leap first here, then there, only to find that you are running along a blind alley. Your friends and family consider that you have become disoriented, or perhaps even worse. They urge caution. They advise concentration. They suggest a holiday. What they seldom seem to understand is that something genuine and authentic is at the heart of it all. But eventually some little event, or perhaps a personal encounter, signals the moment and the direction, and you know that the door has at last opened, even if on to a completely unexpected path. Everything changes. There is inner peace and security of mind, an unshakeable certainty that this is the path to follow. Others may disagree with the decision, but they recognize a new singleness of purpose. You can at last think and discuss rationally, and even though the former sense of urgency remains, you have become an altogether more relaxed and integrated human being.

At about this stage in my inner questioning my mother and father came out to India to visit the Homes, and helped more than anyone else to clarify my thinking and at least reduce the options that were open to me. By the end of their visit I knew that what I wanted to do was to start a Home in India for which I would be responsible financially as well as administratively, with the blessing and approval of the trustees, but not a part of the Indian Foundation. It would be a Home that would concentrate on particular areas of need beyond the normal scope of the Indian Homes, and which as a matter of fundamental policy would never turn away anyone in dire need who genuinely had nowhere else to go. I felt that the place from which this operation could best be mounted was Dehra Dun, 145 miles north of Delhi. The basic requirements, as I saw them, were an existing Home with enough unused room to provide me with a base, and a committee that would agree to my starting the new venture somewhere in the area, on the understanding that I would not compete with their local fund-raising activities. Dehra Dun fitted all these conditions, and in March 1958, the most beautiful of all months in that part of India, I embarked upon my new task.

Dehra Dun is an attractive and peaceful city, almost an Indian Cheltenham, nestling in the narrow plateau between the Siwalik Range and the foothills of the Himalayas. Life is carried on at a relaxed pace, and the city boasts a number of major national institutions, among them the Forest Research Institute, the Geographical Survey of India, and the Indian Military Academy, one of the finest of its kind in the world. It is a city in which flourish flowering shrubs and trees of every kind, and where the climate is not too harsh. Even at the height of summer the temperature drops slightly at nightfall. In winter, though it is cold, there is never a frost. To the north lie the lower Himalayas, beautiful and arresting as their colours change with the movement of the sun and the passing of the seasons. At night one of the peaks, on which is built the hill station of Mussoorie, becomes transformed into a crown of tiny, twinkling lights suspended between heaven and earth. Communications with Delhi are very convenient, with buses amd taxis plying frequently back and forth, and the night train making a pleasant enough journey.

Hardly had I settled in here than two unexpected developments occurred. The first was that the Home itself, which in the initial stages had not been able to find a single patient, began to be inundated with applications on behalf of mentally retarded children, some of whom had been abandoned and picked up from the street, so that we had no means of knowing their names or ages. It became clear that of all the needs in India, probably the greatest was for young mentally handicapped people for whom virtually the only accommodation available was a full-scale mental institution. The Dehra Dun Home, already now full, housed a mixture of elderly and infirm, physically disabled of different ages, and a large number of mentally retarded. Unless further provision were made in the very near future, the new applicants would have to be turned away, either back to the street from which they had come or handed to the police in the hope that they could find an institution or hospital.

The second development was the Dip. I am not quite sure how or by whom I was first told of the Dip, for one could well live in Dehra Dun half a lifetime and not really know that it existed. It was an unsavoury place on the south-western edge of the town that must once upon a time have been a largish quarry. An open drain ran through the middle of it and at the far end was a city refuse dump. It lay fifty yards or so off a small tarmacadam road whose principal purpose was the Police Lines which lay almost equidistant on the other side, and which served as accommodation for police cadets undergoing training. From the road itself the Dip was out of sight. Indeed one would have to walk up to its edge and peer into it before realizing that it contained a cluster of little mud houses with beaten-out milk powder tins for roofing, and that a hundred or more people actually lived in them. On investigating rather more closely, one would become aware that it was in fact a small leprosy colony.

Dehra Dun, like all Indian cities, contains its share of beggars and others in extreme need who frequently live in little groups or colonies for mutual protection, but there was a special reason for the presence of this small colony, so obviously placed so as to be out of sight. Leprosy is particularly rife throughout the hill country to the north, and in order to combat this problem a small but well-run leprosarium had been established in the city. Thus there had started a migration of leprosy victims into Dehra Dun, all hoping for a cure. But, of course, the majority were not cured and, with little prospect of being received back in their villages, they remained in Dehra Dun. Even today, with the availability of powerful drugs, not everyone can be cured, and those who can normally require a very prolonged course of treatment.

Leprosy is still a much feared and misunderstood disease, carrying a stigma and evoking many prejudices in the public mind. In the 1960s this was even more so than today. The growing number of sufferers, in most of whom the disease had reached an advanced stage, caused considerable concern, particularly among the tradesmen, the hotel keepers and the city authorities. It was not that they were unkind or less sympathetic than most men; merely that so visible a presence of leprosy in the city could be harmful to trade and to tourists. (Dehra Dun was the railhead for anyone going to Mussoorie or the mountain areas beyond it.) Rotary took on the problem and in conjunction with the City Council offered to build proper houses with running water, sewage and full facilities in an attractive area about forty miles out of the city. The offer, of course, was not accepted. Leprosy sufferers, like anyone else, want to lead their own lives in their own way, and on no account to be segregated and cut off from ordinary human communication. After a period of negotiation, during which feelings on both sides undoubtedly ran high, sanction was given for the Dip to be converted into a leprosy colony on the understanding that each family, or individual, would be responsible for building their own house. In addition, formal permission was given to the inhabitants to beg for money in the business section of the city on two specified days of the week.

I shall never forget my first impression of this little community, barricaded, as it were from the rest of the town and yet in essence just another section of the city itself, whose inhabitants were owed the same rights and privileges as everybody else. I was familiar with leprosy from our Home for burnt-out cases at Katpadi in South India, and therefore the physical mutilation of feet, hands and sometimes faces, which is so much a part of the disease, no longer struck me as unusual, let alone something of which to be afraid. Even the sheer poverty of the tiny houses in which they lived was not very different from other shanty towns that I had seen elsewhere in the sub-continent. But somehow the combination of such a degree of poverty with the fact of being ostracized had the effect of creating a common solidarity, so that I felt that I had walked into the midst of a very closely knit community. Certainly I was not prepared for the extraordinary and spontaneous warmth of their welcome, nor for their polite but emphatic insistence that I wait for just a moment before entering any further, until they could hurriedly gather together the customary accoutrements of an Indian welcome.

From out of nowhere two or three simple garlands of marigolds were produced. Someone brought out the best available wooden chair, dusted it with a handkerchief and in the process gave it a sharp but discreet knock, presumably to evict any bugs that might have settled into its joints. When this process was over I was asked to sit down, and a simple ceremony followed, with appropriate but short speeches on both sides.

Even more than this it was the remarkable tidiness of the whole colony that imprinted itself on my memory. Everything was as clean as a new pin; in front of each little house – if such a word may be used – an attempt had been made to grow flowers, and in every verandah there seemed to be a home-made hutch either for rabbits or for chickens. The smell that came from the open drain and from the refuse dump at the western end of the houses had bothered me when I first came down the steps, but there was nothing that anyone could do about it and it now seemed irrelevant in any case. I felt a dignity in these people, different from the dignity that one notices in men and women who have achieved something great in their lives, but nonetheless a dignity with a dimension all of its own. It was impossible to sit there without feeling very humble, without feeling that one was in the presence of something noble – an instance of the way the human spirit is able to rise above poverty and even partial rejection by one's fellows. It was impossible, too, to sit there without realizing that one could not possibly just leave and do nothing about it. I felt that I now knew what it was that I had to set about building.

Later I would learn that the leprosy world, in some countries at least, is not always what it appears to be on the surface. For self-protection, individuals form themselves into groups or colonies, which are highly structured and organized, with a wide and well-planned hierarchy of duties. The most severely deformed, for instance, are given the task of begging, while the least deformed do the shopping, even though they may be the more infectious. Such a group will only admit new members on payment of an entrance fee, which may be as high as £75, and provided the member can contribute to the colony's well-being. The group imposes its own disciplinary code and though the system has many merits, it can also be very hard on the member who does not conform. Groups, or cliques, tend to form within the main group, which results in inter-clique rivalries and discrimination, at times even to outright cruelty to a member who falls from favour.

Despite this, there is something specially appealing about the leprosy sufferer, who is perhaps more deserving of our help and understanding than any other category of disabled person, because of the way he is rejected. Once given the opportunity to rebuild his life as an integrated member of society, he is capable of rising to great heights. Our Home at Katpadi in South India is, to me, an outstanding example of this.

It was now clear that help was urgently needed both for mentally retarded children and for those in the Dip. As if to set the seal on the matter, the Forestry Commission of India offered to lease at a nominal rent of one rupee a year a beautiful thirty-acre stretch of woodland, a twenty-minute walk from the Dehra Dun Home. It lay just the other side of the Rispana Rao, a dried-up river-bed of gravel and sand used as a quarry by local contractors except during the monsoon when it filled with water, at times becoming a raging torrent. Admittedly, there were no mains water or electricity, and because the site lay just beyond the city limits there remained the possibility that none would ever become available. But somehow this seemed not to matter.

While I was trying to adjust to the repercussions of this encounter at Durgapur, another more intimate quest was unfolding itself as I gently trod the first steps that would soon lead to my marriage. We had met on a cold February day at Ampthill, just after the first residents had arrived in the still largely uninhabitable house. When someone phoned to ask if a Miss Sue Ryder could come over, I had no reason to suppose that it was anything other than a further, and welcome, offer of help. Probably because I seldom read a newspaper during those busy days, I had not heard the news that was beginning to spread about her total and dedicated involvement since the last stages of the war in Europe in the needs of millions of survivors of the Nazi concentration camps, and about her relief work for all age groups. As she walked through the house asking questions, I knew I was talking to someone with a vocation and a sense of urgency that I had not met before. But there was also something else, something more personal, that for the time being I could not identify. Then, rather to my surprise, she declined a cup of tea and suddenly was gone, leaving me a little off balance and wishing that I had asked more about herself and the challenge that she faced instead of doing most of the answering.

Now, four years later, we were approaching the threshold at which our two lives were to be joined in marriage. With the inner happiness that this unexpected development brought, came the first awareness that deep inside me I felt the need of a partner with whom to share the task of bringing into being the new venture at Dehra Dun. I felt, too, that the fact that the partner I had been given was someone who was experienced in building up an organization from nothing in the face of extreme difficulties would give our joint undertaking a breadth of vision, a freshness of approach and the financial stability that it would need in order to meet our expectations.

We would have been happier still if our respective Foundations, the Sue Ryder Foundation and my own, had been able to merge. But they had each been in existence too long, each with their specific terms of reference and their own separate body of supporters, to make that possible. Each would have to remain separate legal entities, working in its own field, yet complementing the other in its journey towards the same fundamental goal. Only at Dehra Dun, and later in one or two other projects, were we to have the happiness and challenge of working together in full harness.

Raphael, as we decided to call our first joint venture, was conceived as an experiment in building up a community of men, women and children suffering from widely differing forms of disability or deprivation, each of whom would receive the specialized care his particular handicap required, and yet at the same time feel part of one 'family'. To this end we planned to make it not a single Home, as we had always done previously, but rather a village centred round a small hospital which would provide the specialized medical and therapeutic needs of the settlement. The fact that the plan included a hospital would mean that the individual Homes could remain simple and homelike, but their occupants would not lack professional care and treatment.

The site we had been given was virgin forest land covered with numerous Sal trees and areas of thick brush, and apart from the problem of fetching water, a great deal needed to be done before the first residents could be admitted. However, there was a feeling of adventure in the air that made material considerations like these seem relatively unimportant. Two volunteer nurses had come from England to take over the care of the first residents, and out of the blue a most distinguished and cultured Indian widow, Ava Dhar, arrived to ask if she could help full-time and without salary. She promptly took over the post of administrator and stayed until her death eight years later. To her, perhaps as much as to any one individual, Raphael owes its existence. To provide a base from which the nurses could operate and accept the first mentally retarded children, the Indian Army lent three tents, and two others were hired from Delhi. We had overlooked the problem of how to transport four twelve-foot poles as well as the tents themselves the 145 miles to Dehra Dun, but someone came to our rescue and loaded them on to one of the buses that make the journey every two hours. The initial work of clearing the thick undergrowth was undertaken by a team of leprosy sufferers from the Dip who, to the accompaniment of much shouting of orders, frequent laughter and occasional yells of warning, triumph or delight, I know not what, worked almost non-stop for a fortnight.

Today Raphael cares for approximately 300 people in varying stages of need. There is the 'colony' for burnt-out leprosy cases, consisting of little cottages where husband

and wife can live together; the Home for mentally handicapped children and young adults, called Ava Vihar; the 'Little White House' for fit and normal children whose parents have active leprosy or TB, or who may have no home at all; and a small hospital, which includes a long-term care unit and a TB unit. In addition there is a mobile clinic which operates in the Tehri Garwhal area of the Himalayan foothills, carrying out a programme to inoculate children against TB, following up those patients discharged from Raphael and looking for other patients in special need of treatment.

Of all those who reside at Raphael it is the TB patients, I think, who present the most poignant sight. Mostly in their early twenties and often married, all looking so fragile and yet so appealing, they come to us in a terminal stage of the disease. Their homes lie in the remote villages of the surrounding Himalayan foothills where no TB treatment facilities of any kind exist, and where sometimes a two-day walk is needed to reach the nearest bus service. Some of them we cannot save, but many we can. The problem, however, is that the moment they begin to feel better they want to go home to their families and their work. Usually it is impossible to persuade them that unless they can summon the patience to stay another three or four months and consolidate the improvement already made, they will only break down again. Perhaps, though, the fault is partly ours for not having solved the problem of how to make their long and enforced rest in a rather barrack-room ward attractive enough to tip the scales. The Indian government, acknowledging the need, has asked us to increase this wing from the existing thirty-one beds to 250, promising us substantial assistance if we do. But we cannot contemplate such a major extension without being certain that we can handle the complicated medical requirements involved, and ensure its finances. Yet how dearly we would love to do it if only we could see our way. Perhaps step by step we will.

The community that we hoped to create among such disparate groups of people is gradually coming about. For one thing, the juxtaposition of the different Homes within an area of thirty acres has greatly increased the opportunities for mutual help and companionship among the residents. There are long distances to cover, for the land is shaped like a peninsula, and there seems to be ceaseless traffic, some of the retarded children or the leprosy sufferers running errands or taking messages, the doctor hurrying from the hospital to answer a summons, sweet-vendors from the town selling their wares, the occasional snake-charmer and monkey-man, and little groups sitting around deep in conversation. There are workshops where raw cotton is turned into sheets and summer clothes, a sizeable vegetable garden, a barber, a shoemaker, and even a painting and distemper team, all provided by the residents.

Secondly, the presence of some seventy perfectly fit and normal children has given Raphael a new dimension in its standing in the local community. It has removed any feeling of isolation for the handicapped and severely deprived. And because the children mix so freely and so naturally, except with the TB patients, it has brought a joy and a feeling of being part of a real family which only those who have seen it can really describe.

Then finally, and perhaps most important of all, there is the link between those who live at Raphael and the support groups in Australia and New Zealand upon whom, financially, they depend. Given the fact that we were compelled to look outside India for the bulk of the money that would be needed, there were a number of ways in which we could have set about raising it. But what we wanted above everything else, if humanly possible, was to create the same partnership between Raphael and those who provide its funds, separated as they are by some 6000 miles, as exists between all the other Homes and their local supporters and friends. Hitherto, the basis upon which the Homes had been built and sustained was local involvement. Each individual Home had to raise the money it needed by its own efforts. In consequence the Home belonged to the locality, and therefore the residents themselves had a feeling of belonging. The question now was: could that same bond of involvement be forged and sustained between Raphael and faraway, widely dispersed groups and individuals?

Behind this great ideal lies an issue of principle. Our efforts to help someone raise himself to a higher standard of living, are the most effective and the more valued proportionately as *we* become personally and genuinely involved. In this way, and this way only, we begin to see ourselves as partners in a common struggle; he who confronts me in the weakness of his need, and I, who possess what he lacks and to whom he is looking. Not *I*, the giver, and *he*, the receiver, but *us* together, partners working towards the same – essential – goal. To achieve this at all levels and in a myriad different ways until ultimately it embraces the entire human family is the greatest and most urgent task that faces us all today.

In the domestic, local scene, in an undertaking such as our Homes for disabled people where no account is taken of differences of class or race or politics, the matter is relatively simple. The Home is there for all to see, silently beckoning, inviting anyone who will to enter in. Once a personal encounter has taken place another will probably follow. But even if not, then the visit, the pound or two that has been left in the donations box, or the little act of kindness made to one of the residents, will have taken on a personal quality. From now on it will never be quite the same again, the world of human need has been entered, and attitudes have already started to become personalized.

The question now is: how do we achieve this same personalization, this same sense of partnership between communities and nations the whole world over?

To me the overriding challenge that faces us as we move towards the close of the twentieth century, is the need to heal the divisions that afflict us, to remove the many injustices that make a mockery of our common humanity, and to build a world worthy of our dignity. However great a part governments and the United Nations may have to play in this – and up to date their contributions are not particularly striking – we too, as individuals, have an essential contribution to make. We need first and foremost to enter the distant world of the materially poor and deprived sections of our human family in a personalized and significant way, and show that we wish to become partners in their struggle.

This does not necessarily mean physically going out to them. There are many who go and yet who have never become involved in any meaningful way. What it does mean is a changed attitude, a new disposition of heart, and an inner commitment to translate good intentions into action, and then to continue, no matter how poor the return may appear to be. The ability to persevere until the very end is the condition of any real and lasting achievement.

The Ryder-Cheshire Support Groups in Australia and

New Zealand, and the one or two in Britain, have shown that it is possible to form such a partnership, despite being separated by many thousands of miles. To have watched the way these links have grown and strengthened over the years, to be confronted, for example, by a husband and wife in some remote part of Australia who produce a photograph and say with such obvious pride and happiness, 'This is Krishna whom we support', and to see the effect that this has upon Raphael, has been a very moving experience.

Building this kind of partnership, small though it is and restricted to a single community, is not easy. It will not be achieved by some brilliantly conceived and efficiently executed campaign. Rather it is a question of working, patiently to form the nucleus of a well-chosen team, maintaining the closest possible contacts at all levels, and showing by one's attitude and actions that it really is personal involvement that one is seeking, not just a financial contribution to a popular fund-raising scheme. The very fact that it can be done on a limited scale means that it can be repeated in other fields, and on a wider scale.

There is one essential prerequisite. First there has to come the initial decision to act at all, that one little step that launches you forth along the path you mean to tread. The circumstances under which you take this step, and your motivation, are of supreme importance, for people will want to know how it happened, and to be convinced that you really meant it to be the start of a lifetime's journey, not just an optimistic experiment or the result of a sudden whim.

The person who in our particular case prompted the all-important initial step to start Raphael, and gave it sufficient momentum to keep going, was the boy in the steelworks' hospital. Had he been offered a place in the Jamshedpur

Home, or any other Home within reach, his ardent desire to live, shining forth from his eyes in a way I can never forget, would have been granted. But then there would have been no Raphael. As it was, Raphael may truly be said to be his gift to the underprivileged of India, one life exchanged for many, like a grain of wheat planted in the ground.

Chapter Four

A PART TO PLAY

The founding of Raphael marked the end of what one could strictly call the pioneering stage of the Foundation. Never since, amongst any of our Homes, has a major undertaking been started in tents and with no known, or even easily foreseeable, source of funds, and I rather doubt whether it ever will again, unless we should be called to participate in disaster relief. Perhaps trail-blazing is too dramatic a term, but I feel it describes the previous twelve years. Each step was a little further into the unknown, and taken under the compulsion of an identifiable and urgent human need. One side of me felt sure that I was moving in the right direction, but the other was less certain, to the extent at times of wondering whether it could all possibly work, whether I hadn't made a fundamental error of judgement in committing myself as irretrievably as I had. On more than one occasion I remember looking at the gardener, as quickly and expertly he went about his work, and observing that he at least knew where he was going. Whether others in similar situations have also felt such doubts, I do not know. In my case they were never brought about by other people's attempts to make me change my mind, but always arose from within me, and usually when I was alone. Only during my time in Midhurst did they finally cease, leaving me certain that this was my life's work. Even so there remained the question of how I could best achieve it, what should be my precise role in the Foundation. On this issue I was still to have inner questionings and uncertainties, which finally ceased only with my marriage and the launching of Raphael.

The intervening twenty-one years have seen a further stage in our development, one of consolidation. This was a period in which the magnitude of the need became more and more apparent, with the result that there has been an ever-accelerating growth in the number and variety of Homes. In 1981, the International Year of Disabled Persons, there are 195 Homes spread across forty countries and caring for 5000 people. It was a period, too, in which objectives were defined and an organizational structure determined; in which we learned how to work together despite some differing opinions, and each, as it were, fitted into the role for which he or she was best suited. As a result there has evolved a refining of the original concept of the Homes. The modern, sophisticated Home now built, specially designed and equipped for disabled living, and offering wherever possible the privacy of a single room to those who want it, bears little resemblance to the early Le Court. Yet in terms of basic aims and principles, and in the essential spirit that gives the Homes their individual character, closer to that of a family than a structured 'Home', I believe them to be the same.

In size and shape, and in the categories of need for which they cater, the present Homes vary considerably. In Britain the smallest accommodates only six, and the largest fifty-eight. In India and parts of the Far East Homes tend to be much larger; in Canada and the USA they are nearly all small and as personalized as possible. Some are relatively remote, in country or seaside settings, most are in built-up areas, a few are in city centres. The majority care for the younger adult disabled person, but we also have specialized Homes for disabled children, the mentally handicapped, burnt-out leprosy sufferers, and the old and infirm. Some of the Homes provide a very high standard of living and are equipped with every kind of gadget, others are exceedingly simple. At this point I have very quickly to assert that material living standards, though clearly of major importance, mean a great deal less to some people than they do to others, even within the same cultural background. How often have I heard a resident from one of the British Homes go for a holiday to another and say, 'What a beautiful and happy Home this is and what a happy relationship they all have with each other. But how glad I am to be back in my Home.' Sometimes this is incomprehensible to the residents of the other Home: they simply cannot believe that anyone could really prefer 'that dreadful antiquated Home where everyone just sits around and does nothing' to their own modern building. But what is better than being able to share the universal feeling of home being the place where one is most at ease, and to which one looks forward to returning after a holiday or a journey?

The primary objective of the Homes remains what it always was, to provide care and shelter in an atmosphere as close as possible to that of a family, to ensure that each resident is in the environment that meets his, or her, particular needs, and which enables residents to put those faculties which they still possess to the best advantage in a way of their own choosing.

It has become fashionable to define the goal for which all disabled people should be struggling as independence. In the eyes of some, nothing is acceptable short of total independence, in the sense of living an individual life without being beholden to anyone at all. Until comparatively recently I myself have stated independence as being the basic desire of the disabled person. But on more mature reflection I have come to feel that expressed this way there is a danger of confusing the means for the end. It is also an over-simplification of a complex issue. What we should be aiming at is to give each individual person the greatest possible choice as regards all aspects of living. Not for one moment am I disputing the very obvious truth that one of the heaviest crosses that disability imposes is dependence upon other people. Equally, it is self-evident that everything possible should be done to help the person concerned to achieve maximum independence. But between 'maximum' and 'total' there is a world of difference.

Perhaps I should give an example. A woman with severe arthritis in her hand has reached the stage where, with the assistance of a small gadget, she is able to button up her blouse by herself. But it takes her forty minutes to do it, and this is only part of the business of getting dressed. In the eyes of the more extreme 'independent living' protagonists this achievement has brought the person one step nearer the desired goal. But can we truthfully say that it has? Is the person's life richer and more meaningful by virtue of devoting forty minutes' concentrated work on buttoning up a blouse when a helper could do it for her in thirty seconds or less? Ought we not to say that the ideal is to see that the woman is free to choose which she prefers? She might well find that the forty minutes spent in some creative activity, or perhaps just reading the paper, give her far more satisfaction.

In any case, independence is only at very best a relative term, for man has never been able to exist, let alone operate efficiently independently of other human beings. By sharing a common humanity we are all interdependent, so much so that to hold out independence as an absolute goal is to contradict man's essential nature, and beyond a certain point risks becoming arrogance. Rather, the goal should be defined as freedom to choose – freedom, that is, under law. (I am assuming that the law in question is a good law, one which accords with the requirements of natural justice and upholds the dignity of the individual.)

One of the fundamental principles of our Homes is that once a person has been accepted as a resident – there is often a trial period during which both sides are free to change their minds – he has the right to look upon the Home as his for life. The Home will keep him no matter how ill he may become or how much care he may require, unless he is in need of specialized treatment which only a hospital can give. Very occasionally it can happen that someone begins to behave in a way that makes life intolerable, or perhaps unsafe, for the other residents, and then as a last resort it may be necessary to ask him to leave.

To offer security, to enable each resident to feel 'This is *my* home for the rest of my life', with all the rights and the responsibilities that accompany membership of a family, I consider to be the first and most basic imperative of any Home such as ours. If a resident decides to leave the Home and move to a situation of greater independence in the world outside and then finds that it doesn't suit him, or that he can't cope, then he must know that he can come back as soon as a place is available.

Certainly the Home should not act as a backwater, discouraging the resident from lifting himself towards greater self-fulfilment and freedom of action. On the contrary, without ever applying too much pressure, it should seek to stimulate and help each person to achieve his full potential. I have noticed, particularly with those who came from a very dependent situation, that almost immediately a subtle rehabilitation process begins to take place, by being in an environment where the emphasis is on what can be done rather than what cannot. The sight of others more disabled than themselves doing things that they never thought possible; the discovery of how to cope more easily with the problems of daily living – washing, getting dressed, going to the toilet, and so on; the availability of specialized aids and gadgets, and a building specially designed for disabled people; the contacts with the outside world; new relationships – all these and many other factors combine to give the person new confidence and to broaden his horizons without specific exhortation or preaching.

One of the consequences of this process of rehabilitation, to use the term in its broad not its limited, medical sense, is that a number of residents will want to move out into some form of more independent life away from the Home. For instance many decide to get married, either to another resident or to an able-bodied person. When this first happened, some twenty years ago, we were very much taken aback and for a while could not make up our minds what to do, for the two residents concerned could only marry if the Home provided suitable accommodation and this would be both costly and difficult. We could hardly do anything but agree, and in the end the outcome proved very happy.

Little did we foresee what a precedent this would set and how many marriages would follow. Today the provision of married accommodation for disabled people, houses or flats attached to the Homes themselves or separate housing complexes, has become a major part of our work in the British Isles, and is becoming increasingly so in other parts of the world. This accommodation is not restricted to our residents, but is for existing married couples, one partner of which has been unable to continue living at home because the severity of his disability requires more help than he can receive from government or voluntary sources. The able-bodied partner can remain at home to provide this help but in that event he, or she, ceases to be a wage-earner and the family has to depend upon Social Security, which is considerably less than the grant given towards the cost of supporting them at an institution or Home. For most people it is not a realistic income. To create conditions in which such a family can be reunited and able once again to pay their way like the rest of us is a source of special joy.

Out of helping disabled people remain with their families, we have over the past four years embarked upon what we call a Family Support Service. Its purpose is twofold: to provide the kind of help which severely handicapped people need to allow them an independent life in their own homes; and to provide assistance to the family caring for a severely handicapped relative at home and so lessen that person's dependence on the family. In some cases we find that only an occasional visit is required, in others several hours of help each day. The value of the scheme, which we hope will continue to expand, adapting itself as we gain experience, is the relief and sense of security afforded to the family who might otherwise give up under the strain. If a breakdown appears likely, or if an attack of flu or something requires day and night attention, we offer a temporary place in one of the Homes.

I find there is a tendency, in professional and official circles as well as amongst the public, to look upon a residential Home as a place where people are taken out of the mainstream of life and relegated to a passive existence in a sheltered environment. A minority goes so far as to argue that all disabled people, no matter how severe their disability, should be enabled to live independently in the community, either in a house or a flat of their own, as do able-bodied people. If twenty-four-hour care is needed, then society should provide it. If someone says that this is not what he wants, it is said that he, or she, should be educated towards a more positive approach to life. 'Independent Living in the Community', the term commonly used to define this concept, describes the highly personalized and productive lives that many disabled people live, even very disabled people, setting the rest of us an outstanding example of how to turn adversity into something constructive and of great value to society.

The fact remains, however, that there are others who, through temperament, the nature of their handicap, or other personal circumstances, will never be able to attain such independent lives, no matter what finances or supportive services (care attendant and home-help) may be available. There are others again who, as the result of a deliberate choice, prefer the community life of a residential Home and who would look upon every attempt at moving them out into independent living as a disaster. An example is someone living at home with over-protective parents and slowly shrivelling because he is never able to assume any control over his life. There are also those who, in a desire to become fully integrated into the mainstream of life, move into a flat of their own only to find themselves lonely and isolated because they are ignored or rejected by the occupants of the other flats. There are also those whose disability lies so heavily upon them that they do not feel they can shoulder the responsibility of independent living.

There is hardly a single one of our Homes, in whatever part of the world, which does not have its share of residents such as these, who can no longer play an active role, yet who, by their uncomplaining acceptance of their condition and by their dignity, make a lasting and unforgettable contribution to the quality of life within the Home.

A residential Home, assuming it to be run in the way its residents wish, is not just a temporary *faute de mieux*, a kind of stopgap that is tiding us over until the day when society is better organized, but an essential part of the fabric of disabled living. Far from isolating, it integrates those who live in it, because it has been conceived and built by the local community, and exists as part of that community. A good Home grows into a group of individuals who are encouraged and supported in the growth of their individuality, and in the acquisition of the disciplines necessary for living and working together in harmony. In the fullest sense it is a joint venture between the residents and their neighbours, with the result that there is a giving and a receiving on both sides.

At all costs there should be no sense of 'we the staff and administration, and you the residents'. Both should be equal members of the same team, though clearly with different roles and responsibilities. Good communication at all levels must exist, with a workable procedure for participation in decision-making by residents in all that affects their essential interests. How best to achieve this may be difficult to determine, but the dignity of the residents demands that this right is guaranteed.

In this struggle to achieve personal fulfilment all elements of the Foundation and of the local community have a role to play – the central trustees and their small administrative staff, the management committee and its sub-committees, the specialist advisors attached to the Foundation, the GP and the local social services, the volunteer helpers, the support groups and, most important of all, the staff. We soon discovered that it is principally upon the staff and helpers in the Home that the happiness and well-being of the residents will depend. To be able to participate in shaping one's personal future and that of the community of which one forms a part is one of the most fundamental of all human rights, which if denied reduces the individual to a mere unit of society. No matter how skilfully you may organize your administration, or what systems of control you may build in, no matter how successful your fund-raising or how well-equipped the Home, in the final analysis it will all come down to the calibre of your staff and the relationships they establish with the residents.

For a long time we looked to trained nurses, SRNs and SENs, as the backbone of the care staff. But gradually it became apparent that hospital training did not entirely prepare a nurse for the diversity of work in a residential Home, among disabled residents who often did not require the specialized skills of a trained nurse, and who were constantly striving to assert their independence. A hospital nurse could often feel frustrated at not being able to put into practice the full range of her knowledge and experience, and the effort to adapt to so different a routine and method of working proved very difficult in some cases. Only in the case of a nurse who felt attracted to long-term care rather than hospital nursing did the arrangement work.

The aim of a residential Home must always be to find, and

then train, men and women of the requisite stature who will behave as friendly helpers working with, rather than for, the residents. The Head of Care especially must be a leader in the best sense; someone who is ready to take decisions when necessary, but who will try to have as many as possible taken with the general agreement of the residents and staff; someone whose actions are respected by all well-informed people because they are based upon a sympathetic understanding of all points of view. He, or she, should be a catalyst to release the potential in both residents and staff, someone who is sensitive enough and sufficiently competent to respond to the wide range of physical, mental and spiritual needs to be found among even very small groups of disabled people.

These needs may range from those of the uninhibited extrovert who seizes every chance to control the pattern of his own life, and whose attitude often brings chaos to timetables, to those of the residents in the terminal stages of, say, multiple sclerosis who are ready at last to lie back in loving arms. There is also the problem of transition from one stage to another in the same person, which needs to be recognized and unobtrusively and sensitively supported. Then there are residents who may have taken a conscious decision to opt out, to be 'loners', and those who do so because they feel too insecure and too insignificant to participate in the communal life of the Home. Each needs help of a different kind, and the best staff are those with the professional knowledge, the human understanding and the flexibility of approach to be able to provide it.

If the staff are to live up to their calling and responsibility, they need support, accessibility to 'in-service' training programmes, and at times specialized professional help. This comes mainly from the management committee, and the local social and health authorities. It also comes from the central trustees, each of whom has personal responsibility for two or three Homes, and who have at their disposal a full-time team of professionals in counselling, mental care, personnel, architecture for disabled living, specialized aids and gadgets, housing associations, and public relations.

The role of the professional and trained care-staff is vital to the well-being of the residents, but we are first and foremost a lay person's organization. The individual Homes have been started by the local community, and in every instance have become integrated into the community as part and parcel of their life. Ordinary men and women, from all levels of society, have taken responsibility for them and given their time to serve in whatever capacity is needed. My mind is filled with images of so many people, a sea of familiar faces, each with his own story. I suppose because they are the most anonymous, it is the members of the support groups and the individual helpers attached to no particular committee, who stand out. From them comes the bulk of the money to keep the Foundation moving forward. We have as yet never undertaken centralized fund-raising nor employed a paid fund-raiser, but have left everything to local initiative. In Britain alone these support groups are raising over £2 million a year, and the sum increases every year. They do this on a purely voluntary basis mostly by such conventional methods as garden fêtes, sponsored walks, coffee mornings, fashion shows, bring-and-buy sales.

Sometimes their methods are not so conventional. In the late 1960s my wife and I received a letter from a group of children aged between seven and eleven telling us they had organized a sponsored 'shut-up' on our behalf. The vicar, it appeared, had given them the use of the church and, on the supposition that it would last an hour at the most had volunteered himself as invigilator. The parents, having presumably made a similar calculation, had offered twenty pence for every quarter of an hour they remained silent, and as a concession had allowed them books and simple toys. But neither the vicar nor the parents were to be let off quite so lightly. The children had kept quiet for six and a half hours, and collected £165 from their parents. A footnote to the letter added that the noise accompanying their exit from the church defied all description.

All this may sound rather humdrum, but in fact it is a distinctly personal operation, often colourful, marked by great generosity and commitment. On my last but one visit to India, I had just arrived at the Delhi Home when a young, rather travel-worn, Englishman followed me in on a bicycle. I assumed he lived in Delhi and gave him a wave and a nod, to discover that he had pedalled all the way from Lancashire to raise enough money to buy his local Home a bus. Seeing me at the front door he supposed that I was there to welcome him, though how I had timed it so accurately or even known anything about his unannounced arrival he was completely at a loss to understand.

There is another special memory that remains in my mind. A family in North Sydney had 'adopted' one of the retarded children at Raphael, at a cost of £100 a year. They were by no means wealthy, and when two or three years later the father had to give up work because of ill health, they found themselves in considerable financial difficulties. But despite everything they decided that the little girl in India had become too much part of the family for them to give up the sponsorship, and in order to keep it up, the mother, who had never gone to work before, took a part-time job.

In the same way that the strength of the Cheshire Foundation Support Groups lies in the fact that they are appealing for something that is local, for a Home that will be part of the surrounding community, so the lifeline of the Ryder-Cheshire Support Groups is the personal link that has been built between themselves and Raphael. It has taken many visits to Australia and New Zealand, and much hard work and perseverance by many people to make this link a reality, but the effort has been amply rewarded. At the outset there were some who felt that a simple and more effective way of raising the money – currently £60,000 a year for the running costs of Raphael, in addition to all that is needed for constructing, updating and extending the buildings – would be to put it in the hands of professional fund-raisers.

This might perhaps be so. But, given the nature and the objective of Raphael, it was not just money but personal interest and involvement that we needed. We wanted those who work and live at Raphael, unable for the time being to raise their own funds locally, to know that they had a power base, if I may borrow a political metaphor. Only with such a base could they hope to achieve continuity and the means of adapting to the future. In our own eyes the personal links that have gradually been forged between Raphael and the multiplicity of distant support groups, small and large, give the venture a meaning and a stature that no amount of money on its own, however substantial, ever could.

Quite apart from this, Raphael has always been just one step in a journey. We saw it as a pioneer undertaking in how to meet human needs in the developing world which are not likely to be met within the framework of existing organizations. We hoped that out of their experience of becoming

The Homes

*The principal objective of the Homes: to offer each
individual a life of his own choosing*

A Wilderness of the Spirit

Djuriah was disowned by her family because she became engaged against their wishes and was then abandoned by her fiancé after a motorcycle accident in which she was injured but he escaped unhurt

Companionship and Help

(Above) A family outing: grandfather and grandson. (Below) Mutual pleasure: by these small kindnesses are large happinesses wrought

Companionship and Help

From the very beginning the young have been visitors
to the Homes, bringing their own special qualities and life.
Here, mending a wheelchair at Beechwood, Huddersfield

Companionship and Help

The woman is blind and cannot walk. The hut she lives in
is set in a forest on top of a hill, with no-one else closer than a
mile. She depends for her food on the kindness of local people

The Developing World

(Above) The majority of disabled
people in Africa and India are in the rural
areas, but the facilities are
all in the towns. Our great task is to
reach out into the villages if
only we can discover a way. (Below) Africa:
School is two miles away, but
this mother takes her handicapped daughter
every day and still finds time
for her family duties

*Time on his hands. A popular and
profitable occupation throughout the Homes*

Work and Hobbies

(Above) Lusaka, Zambia. The last job before going to bed: tidy up, clean shoes and calipers and stack them in their proper place. A well organised Home run by African and Italian Sisters where the children are made to do everything for themselves and all take pride in doing it. The Home aims to equip the children to take their place in the world. (Below) Dagoretti Children's Centre, Nairobi, Kenya. An African teacher and his pupil. The deaf class was his own brain-child, and for the past five years the focal point of his life

Work and Hobbies

(Above left) Chairs and models out of clothes pegs, with
no hands to help. How Boetie de Wet lifts each piece, positions
and then releases it so precisely with only a rubber tip to
his 'control column', I have never fathomed. (Above right) Selangor,
Kuala Lumpur. Nearly every Home has at least one pet.
(Below) St Vincent's, Limuru, Kenya. Faith, one of the residents,
runs a nursery school for 40 local children

*Oliver and his double bass, on his way to rehearsal at Bamay
Mapagmamal, Quezon City. The Indonesian, Philippine, Caribbean and
West African Homes are outstanding for their music and singing*

Sport

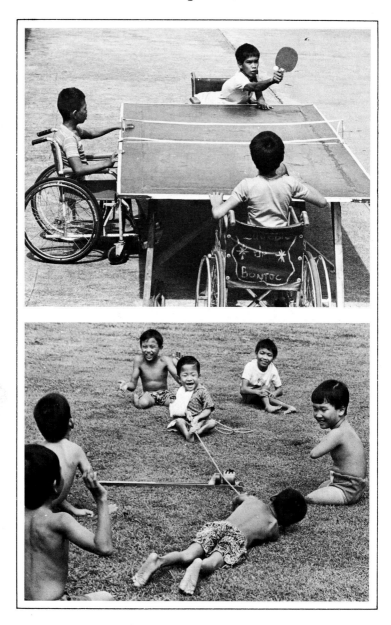

*Sport plays a crucial part in the
young disabled person's life. It develops
innate skills, and allows him
to become competitive and adventurous*

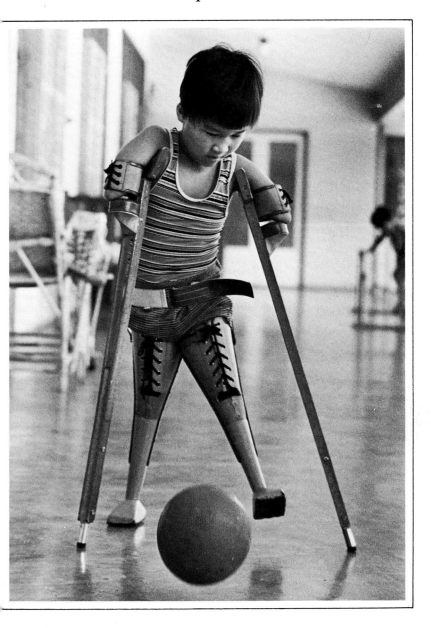

*Kuching, Sarawak. Five year old
Ben-Ben is a born athlete, a good swimmer
as well as a football player*

Leprosy

(Above) Raphael, the Ryder-Cheshire Centre, India. A mother and daughter in the leprosy colony. The daughter is protected at Raphael and will not catch the disease. (Below) A visit to the leprosy colony by the author and his wife

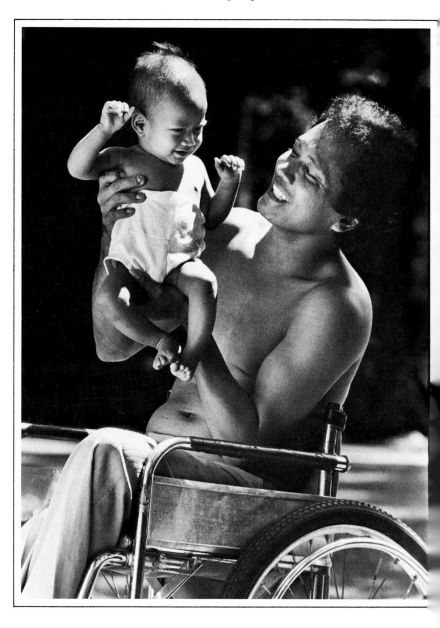

Susano Tansiongco and his wife adopted baby Alvin.
They live in a small hut which they helped build in the grounds
of Pangarap Home outside Manila

personally involved in the struggles of the deprived and handicapped in one corner of a faraway land, the members of our Australasian Foundation would inspire others to become similarly involved elsewhere, and perhaps themselves feel moved to undertake new commitments. This is already happening, in the form of a training centre for the handicapped in Madras, a Home in Kathmandu, and now the starting of local Homes in Australia and New Zealand.

The effect of all that I have witnessed, during World War II as well as since, has been to impress ever more deeply upon me the solidarity and interdependence of the entire human family. Leaders there have to be, and these may appear to rise above their fellow men, but in their hearts they know only too well that what has been attributed to them is in fact the achievement of the team to which they belong.

This is not just a cosy speculative thought but a reality of the deepest significance. It means that we are all involved, all needed, all organically part of the one human family as a leaf is of a tree. It means that every single thing we do, provided it has a good and constructive purpose, is helping our world grow towards its ultimate goal.

Chapter Five

A WILDERNESS TO CONQUER

Whoever finds himself in the presence of physical disability, or indeed any form of human privation, can either let his eye rest on the outward appearance and ponder on what he sees, or he can seek to discover what hidden depths lie beyond. To what extent is it possible to lift the veil of the outward appearance and look into the mind and the heart of the disabled person? What has the impact of his particular disability had upon him as an individual? What were his first reactions when he finally knew the full facts of his particular situation, and in what way have these reactions been modified with the passage of time? It must be clear that there can be no single, general answer to such questions because of the widely differing circumstances of particular individuals. Nevertheless, I believe that there are certain statements that can be made and indeed, which need to be made in order to help towards an appreciation of this profound personal issue.

One of the tendencies of our modern age, particularly in these days of the welfare state, is to fit people neatly into categories. To each category we attach a label, and the moment the words of the particular label are spoken we think that we know in broad outline the character of the person to whom they refer. The habit, one has to admit, is not entirely without merit, at any rate where it is used in a professional or scientific sense by those who know what they are doing. But in the way that it is commonly used, the result is to depersonalize the human individual and if the words of the label infer that he has a problem, to devalue him as well. A clear example of this is to be found in our habit of referring to people who have a disability as 'the disabled'.

The term 'disability' indicates a lack of ability to perform a function or discharge an office, and in its broad sense may be defined as an 'impairment of any of our faculties, whether physical, mental or emotional'. In other words, to be inadequate in any aspect of what society considers normal and reasonable conduct, for instance to have a severe personality defect which renders one incapable of coping with certain social situations, is in the strict sense of the word to have a disability. Let us suppose there are two men who, asked to make an after-dinner speech, find themselves unable to bring it to a conclusion. The first is impeded by a severe stammer, the other, far from being impeded, is spurred on by an incurable attraction to the sound of his own voice. In such an instance we might refer more charitably to the former, but is there any good reason for regarding the first as suffering from a degree of disability and the other not?

Whilst this is not perhaps the sense in which 'disability' is understood in everyday language and may be regarded by some as an unacceptably broad definition, I make the point in order to stress the fact that the distinction between being disabled and whatever we choose to call its converse – non-disabled, able-bodied, normal (the appropriate term eludes me) – is a very fine one.

What we need to remember above all is that disability is just one of those things that can happen to us human beings, and that it does not make us intrinsically different from those who are able-bodied. All of us have limitations which affect in one way or another our ability to function as a fully integrated and reliable person. The fact that we tend exclusively to use the term 'the disabled' instead of 'disabled people' is indicative of an attitude of mind, implying that we look upon such people as forming a distinct and complete group, different from the rest of us and therefore deserving an identifying label. The all-important truth, from which all else proceeds, is that a disabled person is first and foremost a person, a person like anyone else who happens, purely as a secondary consideration, to have a disability.

Those of us who consider ourselves 'normal', in full possession of most of our physical and mental faculties, tend to approach the matter with a number of false assumptions. If we happen to be working in this field, we may well have become so accustomed to seeing disabled people behaving in the way that most people behave, that we take for granted their cheerfulness and their fortitude. But in so doing we overlook the immense inner frustrations, perhaps even despair or anger, with which they have had to contend in order to arrive at the state of mind in which we now see them. We also, I suspect, tend to think that a man in a wheel-chair or anyone who is severely disabled, ought to behave like a saint. In a curious kind of way we put him in what I call the 'stained glass window category', looking upon him rather as a monk enclosed in a monastery – as if a monk did not suffer from just the same temptations as every human being! Those who have had no contact at all with disabled people very often start by looking upon them as if they were a series of wheelchairs, not in any way human beings like themselves. Because they have little idea what to expect, they are confused and ill at ease, and in consequence they may well say things which will cause considerable affront to the disabled person to whom they are speaking. It is in our common interest, therefore, that we should make a determined effort to try and understand something of what goes on in a disabled person's mind.

What is needed is that we remove our gaze from the external manifestations of the disability and look through it to the person who lies behind it, in an attempt to establish a relationship with him and capture something of his thoughts and emotions. In doing this we will begin to see him as a person, with his own share of all that goes with our common humanity, and only incidentally as a person with a disability. We will then see how out of place are generalizations and classifications, and will realize that no two disabilities and their circumstances are quite the same. Disability, as we have seen, may afflict a person at any moment during his life, or even before he has left his mother's womb. It may strike suddenly without a moment's warning, or it may creep up gradually and almost imperceptibly. The disability itself may take any one of a hundred and one different forms, sometimes rendering the person almost totally helpless, sometimes leaving him with a handicap that makes relatively little difference to the course of his life, even though outwardly it may appear to be of a serious nature. Over and above all this each individual is different in the situation and the relationships in which he finds himself, in the way he has accustomed himself to respond to the rough and tumble of life, and in the steps that have been taken by other people to minimize the effect of disability upon him. In any case, what he feels today may be quite different from what he feels tomorrow, either because of some unexpected development in his immediate circumstances, or just because he happens to be depressed today and tomorrow will be feeling on top of the world. It follows quite logically that no two people are likely to react to disability in the same way, and that therefore each needs to be helped to attain his desired goal of freedom and self-fulfilment in a way that takes full account of his particular situation and his unique personality.

Beneath these many external differences, however, there seems to lie, at a profound level of our human existence, a universal need to be accepted and valued for the unique person that each of us is. So fundamental is this need that we are only able to feel fully at home and fully secure when those around us accept us for the person we actually are, with our faults as well as our strengths. If on the other hand, we believe that the people amongst whom we live or work value us only for the things that they like and admire in us, then we can never spread ourselves out and fully relax, let alone blossom to our full potential. If my family or my colleagues do not accept me, then I am no longer free to be myself and to become the kind of person that I know I ought to be in my own good time and in my own way, with the possible result that I will either just shrivel up or openly rebel. If I am physically disabled and dependent upon someone else's support, I have a special need to feel that what is being done for me is not out of a sense of duty, or still worse pity, but purely because I am me. If this is not the real reason behind the help and support I am being given, I am bound sooner or later to sense it, and then there will begin to set in a feeling of loneliness, if not real rejection.

At another level of human experience, most of us want to be appreciated and valued by our fellows for something we have actually achieved. The achievement itself might be something outstanding in any field of human endeavour, or it might just be the fact of having been a good mother. But the fact is that the great majority of men feel a deep-rooted need to know that in some area of their life they have accomplished something for which others will notice and admire them. It is, of course, true that the fact that we have succeeded in whatever we set ourselves to do is a reward in itself. The history of civilization records numerous examples of men of genius who have believed in the value of their work despite never receiving recognition. But for the most part these are the exceptions, and even they must have felt a disappointment, a sense of isolation. To most of us the knowledge that others recognize that we have attained success of some kind is a source of inner strength and comfort, and a spur to help us conquer new fields. Should adversity suddenly strike, it gives us confidence and courage with which to fight back. But the man who has never succeeded, or who always seems to come off second best, may well suffer a crisis of confidence affecting his relationship with others, and will inevitably feel that a dimension is missing from his life.

What, then, can we say of the young person, still on the threshold of a career, his heart filled with ideals and aspirations, who is suddenly brought down in full flight by an accident or a disabling disease? What must his thoughts be, poised as he is to set out in pursuit of success, or adventure?

I have come to feel that herein lies the key to a proper understanding of the impact of disability, or indeed severe deprivation of any kind, upon the human individual. I do not mean to suggest that a young person who has just been told that he will be confined to a wheelchair for the rest of his life, or perhaps even worse, will immediately exclaim, 'Oh, now I shall never be valued.' There will be many immediate problems of an extremely practical and pressing nature to occupy his mind, indeed he may hardly be capable of coherent thought at all. In any case, the need I speak of is so fundamental and deep-rooted that it does not operate in that kind of way. It requires time, and perhaps a measure of calm and solitude, to surface. Even when it does appear it may disguise itself, so that even the person concerned may not quite recognize it for what it truly is. But whether recognized or not, I believe it to be present in every single one of us, as an intrinsic part of our human condition. I believe, too, that if we fail to take it into account in our relationships, and in particular with the disabled person or somebody who for one reason or another cannot quite cope with life, the inevitable result is to make him feel inferior. But these are general points: let me give five specific examples. The stories are all true even if elements have been transposed.

Lenny Dipsell was born in 1925 in Dagenham, Essex, the second son of working-class parents. His mother was never in very good health, and his father worked as a milkman for the Co-op, leaving on his first milk round at four in the morning and his second after a short interval at home for breakfast. Life was not easy for the family. For his first three or four years Lenny was a perfectly normal child, although he seemed to have had difficulty in walking and was always asking to be carried. Then at the age of five he suddenly fell ill, ran a very high fever and in a short space of time went completely rigid. He was sent to the Children's Hospital at Barking where he remained for the next nine years, only occasionally returning to his family for short periods. There was no one available to give him an education, but he was intensely interested in everything around him and by making a thorough nuisance of himself he succeeded in being taught elementary reading.

Just before the outbreak of the Second World War he was in such a state of homesickness that his father decided to have him back at home, but by now his mother's health had deteriorated to the point where she was unable to take Lenny to the bathroom or even to dress him, but had to confine herself to the cooking and housework. She could not do this for much longer as she was found to be suffering from a particularly painful form of cancer and was ordered to bed. There she remained for four long years of pain and grief, watching her husband take over her own duties as well as looking after Lenny. Mercifully, the older brother was in a reserved occupation and so could help in the evenings, but he says that he cannot remember his father ever sleeping in a bed during this time, because of being constantly needed at night as well as by day.

In 1943 the mother finally died and the brother was called up. The father was almost at the end of his tether and as a final straw found that he owed £150 for the doctor's bills and the pain-killing drugs – a very large sum indeed in those days. It was impossible to keep Lenny at home any longer, and so he was sent to the only place available, an old people's ward. To all intents and purposes he was now on his own; the only young person amongst the very old, most of whom were living completely in the past and had been brought in to die. For Lenny, death never seemed very far from the ward.

On many occasions I have sat on Lenny's bed just to spend a few moments together, and asked him to tell me what his feelings were during that period, and what effect it had upon him. Because of his lack of education he found it difficult to give clear expression to his thoughts and emotions, although in fact he was a highly intelligent boy, but the fact that he had to struggle for the words he wanted seemed to give added meaning and poignancy to what he was trying to say. I listened not to a story or a description, but rather to a series of almost disjointed statements, spoken with great feeling, but with no sign of resentment or bitterness. The impression I was left with was of the vigour and hope of youth reaching out to the future, but seeing nothing but the very old and dying, like a man alone and without help in a fearful and desolate wilderness.

I can still hear him saying, 'I know it is wrong to wish one's life away, but that is what I ended by doing.' But his slowly acquired ability to read, and a little later on, to play chess, and such companionship as the nurses and the occasional visit of a social worker were able to give him, kept him sufficiently occupied and sane so that he knew he must not give up hope. He had a remarkable innate sense of humour and longed to burst out into song, for he loved music. This he was dissuaded from doing, because it disturbed the old people, but he would hum away to himself quietly in a corner, and this, too, helped sustain him. Nevertheless, when the hospital almoner, who had been doing everything in her power to find a more congenial place for him, came to tell him that despite all her efforts she had nothing to offer, he felt that he really had come to the end of the road and decided to go on a hunger strike. This was something the hospital had not previously encountered and when, after three days, it was perfectly clear that Lenny meant what he said, they mounted a final effort to find somewhere. This was when they heard of St Teresa's on Predannack Moor. From all accounts it appeared to them a somewhat dubious venture with an uncertain future, but the urgency was such that they felt the risk was justified, and Lenny was put in an ambulance and driven the three-hundred-mile journey to the western tip of Cornwall.

The Home to which he came was a far cry from the one he had left. Drinking water was still fetched from the farmer's tap, and supplying it was a daily duty assigned to one of the residents. Water for all other purposes was pumped by the aerodrome's fire engine into metal tanks that had been fitted into the roof. Electricity would have come from a temporary extension connected to the nearest transformer on the all-but-deserted airfield, but this proved beyond repair, so the Royal Navy Air Station at Culdrose agreed to supply a mobile generator on a 'temporary loan' basis. The drainage system consisted of an ancient but very large tank sunk into a marshy piece of ground, and which had to be emptied by the local council at least once a month. There was a trained nurse in charge of five or six permanent staff and a variety of voluntary helpers, whose efforts were divided between keeping the fabric of the building intact, and providing entertainment and general help for those who lived in the Home. But it seems to be a rule of life that adversity and the common sharing of material difficulties make for an *esprit de corps* that under more favourable conditions may not exist. This was certainly the case at St Teresa's; so much so, that when two years later a new and very attractive Home had been built on an ideal site close to Penzance and the ambulances arrived to transfer the residents, many did not want to leave. No matter what others might think or say, the old St Teresa's had become a home to them in the fullest sense of the word, a home moreover in the building of which they themselves had played a part. Each in his own way had done something to help, either in the daily chores, collecting money, or in renovating the building, mending the curtains or sheets and so on. Until the end of their lives the majority felt nostalgia for what became in their minds a time when they were pioneers, settlers who open up hitherto uninhabited land and make out of it a home and a living.

For Lenny, going to Predannack must have been a bewildering experience, but he proceeded in a remarkably short time to find his feet. The unaccustomed activity and bustle, the companionship of people of his own age and the realization that the Home existed on a very precarious footing had a galvanizing effect on him. He had been brought up to know what it was to have to struggle for his existence, almost totally dependent on other people's help, and now it began to dawn on him that there were, in fact, things that he could usefully do. For a start he was free to sing, and discovered that the other residents enjoyed listening to him. Money, he knew, was probably the greatest need of all, and an idea was beginning to form in his mind. There was an old piano in the Home and one of the residents who had recently arrived, Enid Bottomley, played it rather well. Enid herself was paralysed from the waist down, but perfectly normal otherwise, and was both young and attractive into the bargain. Lenny suggested to her that the two of them should practise a little song and piano act, with a view to putting on a small show in one of the local halls to raise money. The 'concert', as it now came to be called, was scheduled for a winter's evening in the small fishing village of Ruan Minor on the eastern side of the Lizard Peninsula. The helpers who had organized it did not really know what to expect, but they just did not think they could refuse Lenny and Enid.

The curtain went up to reveal Enid sitting in a wheelchair

at the piano and Lenny reclining in his usual position, neither upright nor lying down, but at approximately 45°, his knees bent over his left side, his two hands more or less together below his chin and his whole body as rigid as a board, except for a little movement which could be detected in his left hand. The audience were shocked into complete silence. They consisted largely of fishermen, who in their own way were accustomed to hardship, but as Lenny had very shrewdly judged, they had kind hearts.

For this reason, Lenny decided that he would open the 'concert' by singing one of the more sentimental pre-war hits, *Beneath the Lights of Home*. The fishermen would no doubt have responded well enough whatever he had chosen and no matter how poorly he sang it, for the fact that he was there on the stage at all was proof enough to them that he had courage. But as they began to realize that he had in fact a definite singing talent, and as the words of the song themselves made their impact, carried across the room by this strong young voice, many of them were deeply moved. The concert proved so successful that other villages began to ask for a performance, and throughout that winter Enid and Lenny made more than twenty appearances. At the end they found that their takings were not far short of £590, and these they gave to the Treasurer for his building fund as what they described as 'our thank you for having given us a home'.

I am not quite sure to what extent we realized it at the time, but Enid and Lenny's concerts gave a new dimension and thrust to the development, not just of St Teresa's, but of the other Homes that were to follow. St Teresa's itself was at a critical stage; it could not possibly survive another winter and a new Home would have to be found or built. But how? And where? I myself was in the sanatorium, and the general public knew almost nothing about what a disabled person wanted from life. They supposed that he was someone who needed care and attention, but that this was provided by the National Health Service and that there was nothing that *they* were required to do about it. If you were to talk about the need for a Home which really was as much like an ordinary home as possible and which required the involvement of people like themselves, you would often be met by a response like, 'How dreadfully depressing. Of course, I will help by giving a donation, but please don't ask me to visit or to become involved, I don't think that I could stand it.' Even today there are some who feel the same. Now, suddenly, Enid and Lenny had begun to make an impact on the world outside their Home and to demonstrate that, far from sitting back and waiting for others to help them, they were determined to become part and parcel of the committee's drive to raise funds. More important still, people living in the general area, who would never for a moment have dreamed of coming to the Home, were discovering how like themselves, or perhaps their children, were Lenny and Enid. The impact of their disability began to recede, and some of the prejudices and misconceptions that had hitherto been in people's minds began to fade. As news spread of what was taking place, the little group of men and women in their isolated Predannack Home became not so much the cause of an appeal for financial help as a symbol of human achievement which the local community was proud to look upon as an integral part themselves.

John Prideau's story, however, is a very different one. At the time of his accident he was thirty-one years old, and happily married with two young children. Coming back from work one evening he had walked out from behind a bus and been knocked over by a car, with the result that he became a severe quadraplegic. He was totally paralysed from the waist down, had only very limited movement in both arms and, in addition, had suffered facial disfigurement. For the first month or two he lay in the intensive care unit of the local hospital, where he was fortunate in receiving the best possible medical treatment. There were sophisticated machines by his bed and doctors and nurses in what seemed to him almost perpetual attendance, and the atmosphere was one of competence and professionalism. Although nothing was actually said to indicate this, he began to feel sure that the situation would not turn out quite as badly as it had appeared at first. Whether he would regain all the movement he had lost or merely part of it was never discussed, but nonetheless he found himself buoyed up by the hope that all this expert and expensive treatment must bring some result. His wife was more solicitous than he had ever known her; she was clearly distraught with worry on his behalf, and her daily visits helped greatly in sustaining his morale.

Finally, however, there came the day when he was moved out of the intensive care unit into a bed in one of the wards. Now a new and very different situation began to emerge. He was no longer surrounded by almost continuous care; in fact, at times he was left for the greater part of the day entirely on his own. Whereas in the intensive care unit he had been in the company of others like himself, most of them mentally alert even though seriously disabled in body, here his companions were of a very different kind. They were of all ages, suffering from all kinds of ailments, and appeared to have very little in common with himself.

On the third day the doctor pulled the curtains round his bed, sat down and embarked upon what clearly was going to be a heart-to-heart talk. John heard what the doctor was saying clearly enough, but he was too stunned to take in the real meaning of his words. In fact, he was being told that although the best consultants available had been called in and had tried everything they possibly could, there was now no further medical treatment that could be given. In short, he was never likely to get any better or regain any of the lost movement in his body. The doctor was a kind man and showed that he was not in a hurry to leave. But John was too shocked to know what to think, let alone what to say or ask. Later that evening the real truth of his situation gradually began to percolate through his mind and, despite the extra drugs that had been prescribed for him, he lay awake struggling to find a glimmer of light in the darkness that seemed to have engulfed him.

In the midst of it all a new and completely unexpected doubt began to creep into his mind. As it gradually emerged and took shape, he realized that it had been lying dormant for the past three or four years, though never compelling enough to rise to the surface. To all outward appearances his marriage had been a happy one. His job in the City provided him with a good enough salary, and this, together with some money that he had unexpectedly inherited, had made him a little better off than the majority of his neighbours. His wife was a gregarious person, and liked to entertain and to be seen with her husband dining and dancing at expensive restaurants. He, on his side, was proud of having such an attractive wife, and felt by and large that he was getting on in the world. But had either of them paused to look at their relationship more realistically, they might have asked themselves what they would feel about each other if their married life had been conducted under somewhat poorer circumstances. This, in fact, is what they were each now beginning to do. Confined to a wheelchair and with only very limited movement in his arms and hands, John realized that he had no chance of holding down his job; he would never be able to dance again; and what he would feel like in the kind of restaurants at which he used to dine he did not dare to ask himself.

With a sudden sense of shock a still more urgent question came into his mind. Would he have enough money to pay the housekeeping bills and keep his family at the standards to which they had become used? A host of questions followed. How would he ever get up the stairs to his bedroom? Or into the bathroom, which was down three steps? Here in hospital he could not even put on his pyjamas without a nurse to help him. What about getting dressed at home? He could hardly spend the whole day in pyjamas, nor could he remain in bed. There were more intimate and personal matters, too. He was incontinent and needed to wear a special appliance which had to be emptied and cleaned out once or twice a day. How would his wife take to this? The physical side of their marriage had always meant a great deal to both of them, but now he was no longer an attractive marriage partner. His wife might even experience some repugnance at the thought of touching him, yet he still felt very attracted to her. There was the question of the children as well, the elder of whom had only been kept under control by the knowledge that if he went too far his father would give him a sharp thump. But now this would no longer be possible, and whether there was some other way of successfully handling the boy was very dubious.

The painful reality of these fears became confirmed during the course of the next two or three weeks, when a subtle but nonetheless distinct change came about in the relationship between husband and wife. Nothing was actually said about the more basic issues, only the more immediate and practical ones, such as the reorganization which would have to take place at home, and a rather inconclusive discussion about finance was all the more difficult because no one was able to tell them where they stood in this respect. The husband, who had started by assuming that he would be surrounded by loving care and understanding, and was confident that the principal difficulties would be solved by someone else until he could begin to take decisions himself, now found that it was he who was having to give support and encouragement to his wife. By great misfortune the hospital in question was not well equipped with professional counsellors, and though the vicar, the social worker and one or two others did their best to be helpful, no one had both the time and professional expertise to give the couple the help and advice they so badly needed to cope with the changes in their personal relationship.

The realization that everything he had taken for granted since his wedding day was now crumbling began to build up an inner resentment which soon turned to anger. There was no one he could talk to so he bottled it up, and on the occasions when it threatened to overflow he either disguised it or directed it elsewhere. The more he realized the degree of his helplessness, the more his anger took root. The bus that had stopped where it had, the car which ought to have been travelling a little more slowly, the doctors with all their expensive equipment who, so far as he could see, had done nothing for him, his employers, the neighbours, the very world itself, all in turn became the object of his rage. Had the right person with the proper training been on hand, had his wife been the kind of person to whom he could really unburden himself, this anger could have been worked out of his system and ultimately dissipated. As it was, he became more and more introverted and withdrawn, and despite moments when he tried very hard to pull himself together the whole situation gradually slipped from his control.

The hospital made the necessary arrangements for him to go home, the social worker completed an application form for him to obtain a grant to modify his house for wheelchair-living, and he was told how to apply for a disability pension. For a while it looked as if all might just about hold together, but the truth was that he and his wife had previously each led parallel lives, and it was too late now to forge a union that would see them through the immense difficulties they faced. Having to help her husband to get out of bed, wash and dress himself, cook all his meals and even cut up his meat for him, and worst of all having to accept the loss of her position in the social life of the neighbourhood, was all too much for the wife. Inevitably, the day came when she said that she could no longer manage and that arrangements would have to be made for John to go into a residential home. In her mind the marriage was already finished; she would wait a little while and then leave him.

There are, of course, countless other stories which can be told of wives who have received their husbands back from hospital and given them even greater love and attention than in their previous married life. There are also countless parents who have brought up their disabled sons and daughters and devoted their entire lives to giving them the attention they need. In addition, there are innumerable instances when having a disabled relative to care for has given the family a unity and a spiritual quality that they would never otherwise have had. Yet the traumatic impact that disability has on the individual it strikes is in essence the same for all. What is different are the many factors, external and internal, that have conditioned the individual's response, amongst which, I am inclined to think, the most important of all is that of personal relationships.

The stories of Lenny and John seem to me above everything else to illustrate the role that human relationships play in the struggle to adjust oneself to having become a disabled person. Of Lenny I feel that I can say in all truthfulness that he never entertained any sense of grievance at having been deprived of the normal pleasures and opportunities of life; instead he felt driven by an obligation to live up to the example that his parents had set and to show that he, too, could fight against adversity and deprivation. The scars left by the dreadful experience of more than ten years in a ward of the old and mostly senile remained with him to the end, but never once in the long time that I spent in his company did I detect the smallest hint of bitterness; only gratitude that his circumstances had changed, and a desire to put what remained of his life to good purpose.

John faced an entirely different situation. His parents, though by no means well off, had never had any financial worries. The advent of the welfare state while he was still very young had added to his sense of security, so that he had grown up taking it for granted that his basic material needs would always be provided. Though infinitely better off than Lenny in one sense, he was far less prepared in another for the disaster that was suddenly to overtake him. When his wife left him he virtually gave up the struggle to regain his independence and retreated into his shell, where he remains, an uncommunicative and withdrawn member of the community in which he lives. But this is not to say that he won't suddenly blossom forth into a purposeful and contented being. I have seen it happen in others when I have least expected it.

The change, when it comes, is often startling, rather as if a flickering flame were to burst forth into a great fire, or a crushed reed regain its former suppleness before our very eyes. I went one day to the Head of Home at Le Court, told him that I had a number of tape-recorded talks which needed organizing into a library, and asked if any of the residents could take this on for me. He answered that there was one resident, Peter Courcee, in a wheelchair and suffering from muscular dystrophy, who would be ideal if only he were willing to do it, but unfortunately he seemed to have lost all interest in life and wanted no part in any of the Home's activities. The Head of Home would nevertheless ask him. There was a week's delay before I received an answer, a sort of qualified yes, with a request for detailed instructions.

From then, things seemed to happen so fast that in next to no time I found myself forced into having to apologize for not being able to supply a sufficient variety of recorded talks for Peter to listen to and classify. By now he had persuaded two other wheelchair residents to join him – Tad Polowski, an electronic engineer, and Nigel McKenzie, a journalist, and the 'library' venture soon took on a completely new aspect. They felt that merely cataloguing the talks and supplying recorded excerpts to schools and other organizations on demand did not really justify the equipment they had been given, basic and relatively cheap though it was. What they would like to do was to begin interviewing visitors to Le Court who had something to contribute on the subject of disability, and go out and look for new material with which to expand the library. In order to do this, I was told, it was no use muddling on in an amateur kind of way; a small room must be found somewhere and equipped with proper recording facilities. Le Court supplied the room and the trustees of the Central Foundation allocated a grant. Peter and his team managed to collect the balance, in addition to enlisting the help of the local radio station. Once this had been achieved, their sights were set on producing a quarterly 'magazine', recorded on cassette and comprising a wide variety of topics likely to be of interest to disabled people, interspersed with music very much on the lines of a real radio magazine programme. The studio has now been moved into still bigger premises and is one of the special features of Le Court, always searching for new ideas and more work. I had just finished writing this when, after a short illness, Nigel died. So many people came to the funeral, in the Church of England chapel at Le Court, that they overflowed across the entrance hall and out on to the forecourt.

Peter Courcee has flown the nest. He is married to Kay Simpson, and they are busy building themselves a new life in a council house at Lindhurst only six or so miles from Le Court, close enough for him to keep in touch and still be looked upon as part of the family. To me he stands out as a very special person. He not only came willingly to my help when I badly needed it, but did so with a combination of modesty and great competence and humour, which have made me always look forward to my 'studio' visits. But he is also one of a great multitude, each of whom in his, or her, special way has demonstrated that no wilderness is so barren or so vast as to be beyond the power of man to cross, if he has the will and if there is someone to share, however distantly, his struggle.

I can never forget, either, the story of Gerry Fisher who, when he entered our Essex Home at the age of sixteen, was what I can only call in a state of open rebellion. To the staff and management committee, who I might add became remarkably fond of him, he presented a near nightmare. His every thought and action seemed to be directed towards disrupting the running of the Home's routine and a complete refusal to cooperate. There was much discussion as to what could be done and many attempts at talking him round, but nothing worked until Mrs Timson, the chairman's wife, persuaded him to take up painting. The nature of his disability made this very difficult and at the beginning all he did was paint numbers, but he proved a remarkably apt pupil and before long he developed a style of his own. It was a primitive style, stark and direct, which startled, occasionally even shocked, but Mrs Timson recognized his latent talent, persevered with her instruction, and asked the Colchester Art Guild to arrange a public showing of his work.

Gerry by now was noticeably a different person. He had found a hobby and a purpose on which to focus his energy, and whatever it was that was burning inside him – his frustration, his sense of grievance, his anger against society – at last had a means of escape. In a short time he had changed from an *enfant terrible* into a mature, integrated person who until his death in his late twenties, occupied a place of special honour and respect in the Home. In a sense his life adds its own individual testimony to the role that painting, indeed all art, can play in the building up of man and his ascent towards the spiritual heights for which he is destined.

Both Peter and Gerry, during the time that they were struggling to adjust to the reality of their handicap, were living in a secure and strong relationship with those around them, and this must have helped. However, I have to admit that my general assertion that a good strong relationship is a great help in the process of adjustment, and an insecure relationship the reverse, needs qualifying. I know of one instance at least where an out-and-out hostile relationship served not to depress and hold back the individual concerned, but rather to galvanize him into action.

Andrew Holmes, like Peter, was born with muscular dystrophy, though its symptoms did not really come to light until he was seven years old. His mother died at an early age, and by and large Andrew's early years were fraught with difficulty. Andrew was well built and gave the impression of a strong and forceful man, though in fact the disease had left his arms very weak and he soon became confined to a wheel-chair. Nonetheless he showed remarkable initiative and determination. At school he tried to participate in every-thing, but found it so difficult that he left at fourteen and went to work for a friend who ran a hotel. His job was preparing vegetables, washing-up and, of all things, helping with a conjuring act which his friend did to earn extra money. This was the happiest period of Andrew's earlier life, but unfortunately was not to last. His disability was becoming even more severe, and, despite his friend's pleading with him to stay, he decided that in order not to impose on his friend he should leave the hotel. A few years later, on his father's death, Andrew went to live with his sister and brother-in-law, both of whom had promised the father on his deathbed that they would look after him. Andrew could no longer get himself in and out of bed and had to rely almost totally on other people. Unfortunately his brother-in-law began to take a dislike to him, largely on the grounds that he considered that his wife was paying more attention to

Andrew than to him. They would argue angrily about him, often late into the night, but the sister was not fully fit herself and it was her husband who usually had the last say. Finally it reached the stage where he refused to allow Andrew into the living-room, which meant, amongst other things, that he could never watch television. In addition he set about making life as uncomfortable as he possibly could for him, and before leaving the house, if the weather was cold, he would throw open the window and leave Andrew for hours on end in his room. His arms were strong enough to operate his wheelchair, but he had no hope of closing the window nor of opening the door and moving about the rest of the house. If Andrew provoked or annoyed him, which he tended at times to do, his brother-in-law wouldn't hesitate to hit him in the face.

The only effect of all this, however, was to make Andrew absolutely determined not to give in, and by hook or by crook to get the better of his brother-in-law. What saved him was that he started to go to the occupational therapy centre in the local town where he packed shampoos, working for six hours a day, five days a week. If ever he felt he could no longer cope he would flatly refuse to go home at the end of the day and on those occasions was temporarily housed in an old people's home. Eventually he came to one of our Homes, and within two years married one of the residents. They lived together in specially adapted accommodation in the Home, overjoyed by the new sense of fulfilment their marriage had brought them until Andrew's death a few months ago. If questioned about his duel with his brother-in-law he would speak with a good deal of feeling, but, like Lenny before him, without any obvious bitterness or resentment. Rather, he considered that he had been put to the test and that out of respect for his father, it was up to him not to be defeated but to do his utmost to come out on top.

At the outset of this chapter I said that, notwithstanding the essential differences of each disabled person's character and circumstances, there are some statements of general application that can be made, and indeed which need to be made if we are to attain any understanding of the impact of disability on the individual. Whilst fully acknowledging the limitations of my experience and realizing that not all will agree with me, I now want to offer my considered view of the principal emotional stages through which the average person has to pass following severe disablement. In doing this I am thinking particularly of the younger person between adolescence and, say, the mid forties, for his situation is different, I feel, both from that of the child who grows up with disability from birth, and from that of a person who has thirty years or more of working life behind him before becoming incapacitated. The catastrophe of disability is at its most severe when it strikes in the late teens, a time of life when the person has not yet embarked upon his career, or has only recently done so.

There are, I believe, three main phases through which such a disabled person passes. There is the moment when the person is told, or perhaps becomes aware through his own deductions, that there is nothing more to be done and that for the rest of his life there will be no improvement in his condition. At this stage I find that the response may be anything from panic to sheer disbelief; in some cases the implications of the discovery do not penetrate the mind at all. Inevitably, there will be a number of factors that combine to influence the individual's reaction, for example the severity of the disability, the person's make-up and character, his family or social circumstances, the advance warning that he has been given, and, perhaps as important as anything, the manner in which he is told – or, I have to add, not really told at all. Occasionally the person who imparts this information will do so in a surprisingly abrupt manner, a phenomenon that I have noticed on more than one occasion with professional people not only of high standing but also of deep compassion. I think the fact is that they are acutely embarrassed, possibly even a little panic-stricken themselves, at the thought of having to give such devastating news to another human being.

Once this news has been absorbed and the initial reaction overcome, there follows, I believe, a mourning for what has been lost; something very similar to the way one mourns the loss of a close and loved relative. For many this may persist, possibly throughout their entire life. Time is a gentle and merciful healer, but how many of us totally forget the loss of someone who has been very dear to us, no matter how many years have passed?

Hard on the heels of this mourning, perhaps almost simultaneously, comes the inner revolt – the frustration, the anger, the resentment, the incomprehension at what has happened. One can almost hear the cry: 'Why me? Why at this very moment in my life when there was so much waiting for me to do, or enjoy?' It may well be that there are some individuals who do not suffer this internal conflict, who accept instantly the inevitability of their situation and who adapt totally. But I do think that we need to beware of judging too quickly by the outward appearance. Even some of the saints were unable at first to accept the apparently incomprehensible catastrophes that overtook them. In time, however, they did, and thus, one feels, it was the winning of their inner struggle that made them even more saintly, carrying them along the road towards the full stature of perfection, which all of us are intended to attain. I personally find it difficult to believe that any but a tiny minority, no matter how great the strength of their character, nor how all-embracing the love with which they may be surrounded, are not deeply affected in the inmost core of their being.

Johnny Moore, of the early Le Court days, says that he has had to struggle against frustration all his life, for instance, when a fuse blows, and because he has no hope of reaching it, he is obliged laboriously to explain to his wife what to do; or when a restaurant turns him away because 'the tables aren't suitable for wheelchairs'. He, though, has disciplined himself to adapt. He knows it is his only hope, difficult though he still at times finds it, and in consequence he has risen steadily in the firm he joined thirty years ago and has managed to buy his own house. One of his greatest assets is his policy of looking relaxed and confident in a difficult situation. Many people have stated that if someone in a wheelchair enters a restaurant that does not usually have wheelchair guests, the conversation will momentarily stop and the diners look embarrassed. But Johnny says that this has never happened to him because he goes in with a smile and looking happy.

Yet even here I realize that I need to be careful. I know a Scotsman severely disabled at the age of twenty in a motor-bike accident who is adamant that he never felt anger or experienced any inner conflict. He attributes this to the fact that he had done a kind of Outward Bound course whose motto was: 'Seek, Strive and Never Yield', and that he kept repeating these words to himself day after day. He also adds that he found himself so preoccupied with learning how to manage a wheelchair and overcome the other restrictions to his mobility that he had no time to brood. On the other hand he says that everyone else in hospital with him was very definitely angry in one way or another. One reacted to everything that happened by simply roaring with laughter. All day, apparently, he just laughed.

The revolt that the majority of disabled persons feel at the time that the full implication of their disability settles upon them may take very different forms, but one of the most common is apathy and withdrawal. The person will argue to himself that the disability is not of his doing, and not in any way his own fault; his response, in effect, is to say, 'To Hell with everything.' He will hate the world, resent the confinement of his hospital ward, begrudge the freedom and the mobility of those who come in and out, and make up his mind that under no circumstances will he do anything to help himself, accept any advice he is given or cooperate in any way at all. Very often the disguise is effective, and may be veiled by polite behaviour. Such correct conduct may, in my view, be a danger signal, for it is possible that hidden beneath the outwardly polite appearance may be germinating the first seeds of despair. And of all the possible reactions despair is unquestionably the most dangerous. When a man despairs he loses faith in himself and in his fellow men and, most disastrously of all, in the goodness of God. He is a man who, absolutely and literally, has reached the end of the road, and who more than anyone else is in need of human understanding and urgent help. But mercifully, in my experience, this is the least common of all reactions.

The commonest form of revolt, as I term it, is probably anger, again in many differing forms, but often plain outright anger, undisguised and, at times, violent and unpredictable. Without any apparent reason, it may direct itself against almost anybody, against the nursing staff or the doctors, the husband or wife, even the casual passerby or possibly just society in general. It is not really aimed at the person it hits, but against the disability itself, and the sense of injustice that this evokes. The person who finds himself in the line of fire is chosen merely because the real target is immune and unhittable. It is very important that we understand this and the reason for it, for otherwise we too may fall prey to a sense of injustice and hopelessness, and begin to wonder whether there is any point in our continuing to try and help.

A complicating factor at this particular stage is that the person concerned will find himself deluged by a great number of practical problems and doubts similar to those that John Prideau had to face. Time may not be on his side, for if he is in hospital or a rehabilitation unit his bed will be required and pressure will be exerted to make him move somewhere else as soon as possible. Where is he to go? If home, then how will he manage? What alterations will need to be made to the house? Who will look after him? What will happen to his independence and freedom of choice? There are countless, unforeseen problems of a practical nature that will flash before his mind, possibly adding a note of fear or confusion to his inner conflict.

For the most part this calls for a trained counsellor or social worker who has the necessary knowledge of what help is available from Social Services and from voluntary agencies, and who can discuss these practical problems with the disabled person in a knowledgeable and professional way. Such a person is not always available, whether through lack of funds in the Health Service or through the particular circumstances in the hospital or rehabilitation unit. In consequence, severely handicapped people can find themselves discharged and returned home, or perhaps to some form of residential home, with a great many of these urgent problems unresolved, and perhaps even without the opportunity of exercising any personal choice as to where to go. All this can lead to not only great resentment which later may be difficult to disperse, but also to much unnecessary anxiety and hardship.

For our part, assuming we are a friend or a relative, or somebody engaged in some aspect of caring for the person, our objective should be to try and help him work the sense of grievance out of his system. Whatever form the 'revolt' may take, the worst thing we can do is to attempt to ignore it and to adopt an 'all is fine' attitude, talking cheerfully about this, that and the other, anything, in fact, so long as it does not bear upon the central issue itself. We should be at his side to give him all the comfort we possibly can, and to show that, in so far as lies within our power, we want to identify with his struggle. But this is not the moment to attempt to preach to him, and on no account should we try to tell him that God knows what is best, that behind it all there must be a meaning and a purpose, or words to this effect. The time may come later for gently lifting the conversation to a more spiritual level, but with the majority of people this must be at a time of their own choosing. For the moment it is companionship and understanding, and availability to run an errand that are needed. We should try to make him feel secure, and work to establish a personal relationship in which he feels that he can say anything he likes, no matter how much bitterness it may contain, secure in the knowledge that we understand and will not judge him.

Our part is not to lose faith in him, not to lose faith that the end result, however long it may take, will be a regained sense of purpose and a greater maturity and deeper peace. But in the meantime the battle is at its height. It must be firmly fixed in our minds that it is a battle from which there is no escape. We must know that unless it is won the person will never succeed in quelling the revolt, and thus be able to create the conditions under which he can build a new life.

Chapter Six

THE LAST ENEMY

Not all of us find it easy to talk about death, or even to apply our minds to it with any seriousness. That I now do so does not mean that I am any different, only that death, so frequent a visitor during the early days of Le Court and St Teresa's, is too integral a part of the story I want to tell for me to ignore it.

Despite all the death and destruction that I had witnessed during the war, Arthur introduced me to death in the sense of a personal encounter. The first indication that his death was approaching came in the early afternoon of a warm and sunny August day when Arthur called out to say that he wanted to go to the toilet. Despite his by now almost unbelievably wasted and skinny body, he still insisted on using the commode instead of a bedpan even though he could not get out of bed on his own. On this occasion we were halfway back to his bed when he suddenly stiffened and looked as if he were going to collapse. Rather misguidedly, as I have since thought, I told him not to worry, just to let himself go and relax, and without waiting for a reply made to pick him up. Instead of letting me do so he tried to resist, with the result that he suffered what I supposed to be an internal haemorrhage and cried out a rather agonized 'Lumme'. It was obvious as soon as I had got him back into bed that something serious had happened and that death could not be very far away. I telephoned the hospital to ask what I should do, and received detailed instructions as to how to ensure that death had occurred and how, after a three-hour interval, to lay him out. They did not think I need send for the doctor at this stage, but he would have to come later to certify the death. I then contacted Father Clarke, the Catholic priest, who arrived at about seven o'clock to administer the last sacraments. It was midnight when Arthur died.

Throughout the nine hours or so that I sat with him, the two of us hardly exchanged a single meaningful sentence. Arthur was conscious and leaning against his pillows, which I had arranged as comfortably as I could, but he gave the impression of hardly registering my presence. For my part I felt completely at a loss to know what to say or do. It had been evident for some time that this moment would come, and I suppose that I had tried to picture what it would be like and what I ought to say, rather piously hoping that I would find something edifying or uplifting. But now that the actual moment was upon me, I realized my total inadequacy. The best I could manage was, 'Is there anything I can get you?' or 'Would you like a cigarette?' Arthur would turn his head and look at me, but so far as I can remember he never answered. Indeed I began to suspect that the occasional remarks I was making were a distraction, and an intrusion upon something very personal that was taking place inside him.

Although by now only semi-conscious and becoming steadily weaker, his expression was thoughtful and intelligent, with a certain puzzled look in his eyes. For all the world he was a man holding a conversation on a matter of unusual importance, but it was not to me that he was talking, nor was I in any way connected with the mysterious inner dialogue that absorbed his thoughts. It slowly dawned on me that what he was in fact doing was facing up to a decision. Yet there was an element in the making of it that evidently surprised him, for which he appeared not to be prepared. I had had occasion to watch him closely as over the past three months he had steadily regained his faith, and had been greatly impressed both by his serenity and by the simple, yet authoritative way in which he could answer profound questions about his religious belief. A humble man, he had faced his impending death in a way that was totally convincing. Whatever may have lain in his past, he was now a man of faith in the best and truest sense. Yet, he was now confronted with something that mystified him, something, I had a feeling, that was calling for a difficult choice.

The only words he spoke, or at least the only ones I can remember, made the issue still more obscure. With an air partly of wonderment and partly of deep thoughtfulness, he turned towards me and said, 'Yes, I suppose I shall have to go.' For many years I pondered over those words in an effort to understand what they signified, but without success. Only recently, in the light of what I have experienced since and of what others have written or told me, do I feel that I can begin dimly to see. I can only put this into words, however, if first I make one or two statements about the nature and the ultimate destiny of man as I see and believe it to be, as a Christian.

What distinguishes man from the animal world, even the highest of the primates, is that man is both nature and person. Over and above possessing a nature common to his species, as with all other forms of living beings, he possesses an individual personality, the unique 'I', which makes him different from every other person that ever has been or ever can be. His human nature might be compared with the wood on which a sculptor works in order to produce his masterpiece, and his personality with the sculptor. His life's task, seen from the point of view of his own eternal destiny, is to mould his particular share of human nature, with all its faults and weaknesses as well as its grandeur and beauty, into the unique masterpiece that God has willed. This means that he has to build himself into a fully integrated being, his faculties developed to their fullest potential, his emotions and passions subjugated to the rule of reason, and reason in its turn submitted to the infinite wisdom and love of the Creator's dominion over all His creatures. Only in this way, when the divine life of grace infused into him by God has been able to penetrate and transform his whole being, can he be ready for the life of glory, like a seed that finally blossoms forth into a most beautiful flower.

But man is not just a lonely individual, he is an integral and necessary part of humanity. His lifelong struggle towards self-realization and perfection are not solely for his own benefit, but for that of the human family. What individual man has to achieve in respect of his own person, mankind has also to achieve for itself. It, too, has been given the task of working towards ever greater unity and perfection, until finally, when time has run its course and all is at last consummated, it acquires the cohesion and the harmony that we see in the human body itself. Remote and impossible though this may appear, mankind's ultimate destiny is to become as if a person in its own right, capable of corporate thought and action, yet without detriment of any kind to the freedom and individuality of its separate members. The

Christian calls this the mystical body of Christ – Christ the head, we his members.

Even this is not the whole of man's task. He has been called to master and control the created world and to give it harmony and meaning until it too, in some way that we cannot now comprehend, becomes eternalized as an organic part of the ultimate life and environment of mankind – in scriptural terminology, the new Heaven and the new Earth. We are here and now, in our daily work, in our relationships with other people, in everything we do or think or pray about that is morally good and upright, building eternity. One day we will see the work of our hands, like ourselves, transformed and eternalized by the power of God's Holy Spirit.

We may not be able to picture the achievement of such a cohesion of the infinitely diverse elements of creation, but if we think back to the origin of the world, forming as it did just a single organic mass, and contemplate the change that one little particle has undergone in the intervening 3600 million years, ought we not to be very careful before prejudging what might or might not be a few million years hence?

Or again, if we contemplate what happens to such an ordinary-looking particle as a seed when it has been planted in the ground, should we really be surprised at anything that concerns the future of a living organism? Man sows and cultivates, but it is not he who effects the astonishing transformation into a finished work of art, wholly unrecognizable from the original seed, yet organically one and the same. Is it then contrary to reason to claim that what is constantly happening before our eyes at one level of existence cannot be imperceptibly and silently happening at a higher level?

Under the best circumstances this twofold destiny would

constitute a most daunting and difficult task, but the conditions under which we are called to achieve it are far from ideal. At the earliest dawn of our human family's birth, mankind took a conscious decision not to accept God's dominion. Leaving aside the thorny problem about who exactly was Adam and at what stage in the evolution of man he lived, God asked of him something that seemed either incomprehensible or else in flat contradiction to the destiny he and all mankind had been promised. He decided, therefore, to reject it and take the reins in his own hands. Like so many of us he thought he knew best. Because the way God proposed was so different from how he saw things, he failed to make the supreme act of faith which was being asked of him, and lacking faith he fell back upon the light of human reason as his only guide. Having done this he excluded any possibility of ever attaining the eternal destiny to which he, and the whole of mankind with him, had been called. Moreover, by his act of rebellion he allowed a principle of evil to enter the world bringing in its train disorder of every imaginable kind, physical as well as moral and spiritual.

Since that most fateful of all days, every one of us has become infected by the same virus, and every one of us has added our own personal contribution to the totality of discord and lawlessness with which human history has been marred. Within ourselves we see the evidence of that same conflict, our lower nature struggling to gain control of our higher self, unable to do the good that we would and all too often doing what we would not.

If we have faith, without which it is impossible to attain our destiny, we all too easily build our own picture – caricature might be a more accurate word – of who God is, so that He becomes the God of our own fashioning, not the God of reality. Faith is only truly faith when it has as its object the true and living God as He really is, and when it commits the whole man, body and mind and soul, to His service.

But if our faith has been lacking during our lifetime, there still remains the hour of our death. Only when we have lived through that hour will the story finally be brought to an end.

Death is the final and crucial consummation of that lifelong process of self-determination and struggle for perfection. It is the bringing to maturity of all that a man has made himself during his lifetime, the taking possession without possibility of self-deception or ambiguity of his own personality as it has been developed through the conduct of his life, and most particularly in the domain of his freely expressed moral acts. As such it is an act of the profoundest meaning and consequence, which gives an irrevocable direction to our life for all eternity.

In our dying, no matter what our life has been, saint or sinner, and no matter what our personal belief or faith – Christian, Moslem, Hindu, Buddhist, atheist to the very core of our being or whatever else under the sun – we are all given a last opportunity to accept or reject our eternal destiny. We will find ourselves face to face with reality, that is to say the totality of creation both material and spiritual, and either decide that we wish to become a part of it, or else, whether through defiance, hatred, or insuperable pride, I really cannot conceive what, we turn our back on it to our eternal ruin. Our dying will either be a deliberate and calculated refusal of the invitation that God still offers, or a humble submission to the living God whom during our lives we have only imperfectly known, and still less perfectly obeyed, and who now calls us to a supreme act of faith.

In order to make that act of faith, there is a journey that we will all in our turn have to take, unless by some great calamity we refuse to do so, choosing instead that abyss into which the man who cuts himself off from God falls. For some the journey may be short, for others long and dark. But it remains only a passage. As gold emerges pure and refined out of fire, so will we emerge out of that mysterious test of faith perfected and transfigured, at peace with creation and with God, and co-builder with Him of the new Heaven and the new Earth.

The fact that a man may die suddenly and without so much as a moment's warning will make no difference. God, who created time to be at the service of man, is more than capable of stretching what to us appears no time at all into whatever is needed for a man to make his final choice and consummate his life. All of us have our own particular life to live, and our own particular death to die. For each it is a life and a death that, in a way we cannot yet comprehend, is essential to the building up of the human family to its full stature and ultimate perfection.

So, I think, it must have been with Arthur. At the hour of his dying there was a mysterious inner act of faith that he was being called to make, a particular journey which he was being asked to make, the purpose of which he could not for the life of him see. The words I had heard him speak, and which at the time had so puzzled me, were the external expression of his inner assent, his fiat.

In the four years that were to follow Arthur's death, it befell me to sit beside a considerable number of others during the closing hours, or days, of their lives. Writing as I do thirty years later, I cannot claim to have retained a perfect memory of even the majority of these vigils, though some stand out very vividly and poignantly in my mind. Those who came to old and rather dilapidated house, Le Court, were of many ages, suffering from a wide variety of illnesses or disability, and professed all kinds of different religious beliefs, some having none at all. Occasionally the end would come very suddenly, catching the sufferer as well as myself unawares, but by far the majority lingered on for a long time. Quite a number held on to life with such tenacity ı three if not four days after the doctor had said that the end must come at any moment ı that this will to live pursued to the utmost limit of human endurance is one of my most lasting impressions. Yet in some cases I felt that it was not merely the will to live which kept them going but the fact that beneath the external struggle there was taking place another of a different order altogether.

I acknowledge freely that not all feel they can go on to the very end in this way and that some, either in advance or at the actual moment, see the shortening of their lives as an option they can legitimately take. I fully understand the dilemma and I respect the sincerity of the desire not to be a burden to others, but I can find no basis for the claim that to choose one's own 'exit' is to impart a dignity to one's dying that would not otherwise be there. Everything I have seen and experienced tells me the reverse. It tells me that it is precisely in enduring to the end, with whatever our own individual death involves, that the dignity we have already acquired in life is brought to full maturity. It tells me also that if this goal is to be achieved, everything possible has to be done to alleviate physical pain and mental anguish, and to provide whatever companionship may be needed.

Some, I am afraid to say, died in great pain, for we did not have the facilities and drugs which today can to so great an extent relieve physical pain. It was these men and women who affected me the most, because of the dignity that shone forth from them and the remarkable sense of humour that many managed to retain. Indeed, I have come to think that the ability to smile, even to make some little joke, and thus break the tension for a moment, is a great relief in moments of severe trial. One or two were openly aggressive, and at first I was bewildered, wondering what I had done to provoke them, until I realized that it was not really me they were attacking, merely that they needed an outlet for their feelings. Others undoubtedly found it difficult to look death in the face and to accept the inevitable, and these needed a companion to give them reassurance and support.

The friendship which had been forged between Arthur Dykes and myself during the three months or so that we spent together helped me and prepared me for the others that were to follow. Nonetheless I continued to feel most inadequate. A priest or a clergyman, I felt, would have done so much better. The little word of spiritual comfort at the moment that it was needed would have come so readily to their lips, but this was not so in my case. I was afraid that no matter how carefully I trod or how sure I was of what I was saying I would sound false and artificial. Instead I fell back on the only things that I knew I was able to offer – companionship and being on hand whenever I was needed. The house had no bells, nor even electricity, and because for many the night seemed to be the loneliest, I took to putting a mattress outside the person's door and giving him a little hand bell with an assurance that I would not mind how often he rang it. As with Arthur, I found that merely being available and giving the impression that nothing else in the house really mattered at that particular moment except himself, or herself, and their own individual need, even if at times this was a difficult impression to give, created a true and personal bond. I also found, as so many others know even better than I, that physical contact – holding the other person's hand or supporting his head, provided it is a sincere and genuine act and accepted as such – can be a source of great comfort and at times more meaningful than the spoken word. But above everything else I regard time as the best gift one can offer. Time just to sit and share.

In our present Western society time seems to be a precious and rare commodity. We are all too ready to respond to another person's need by *doing* something for him, perhaps driving a long distance to perform an errand, or to sort out a problem. But just to sit with someone for two or three hours for no obvious purpose, other than the fact that this is what he wants, we look upon altogether differently. The same can be said about good works and prayer. How easy to fill the day doing something, the object and the results of which we can plainly see. How difficult to put to one side even part of the day for prayer or contemplation, without which we may just be rushing around without any clear understanding of the real track we should be following. The person who wants us to sit with him, and who will almost certainly be too sensitive to press his claim, may well be feeling at that particular moment that there is no point at all to his life. What he seeks is reassurance, and if we are willing to give him an hour or two, then our presence alone can give him the reassurance for which he is looking; it is proof that his life means something.

The fact that medical caution errs on the side of withholding news of a fatal condition from the patient, compounded by our reluctance to talk about death, particularly with the person towards whom its finger is already pointed, means that so many, at the very moment when they most need human comfort and support, find themselves isolated and intensely lonely. Their friends will spend half an evening passing on the news to others and saying what a dreadful thing it is, but they are loath to spend that same length of time with the person himself. If they do, then they will go to great lengths to avoid the dreaded subject, turning the conversation into safer and more pleasant topics if ever they feel they are getting too close. It is curious that people who in other situations are such good judges of what impact a particular statement is likely to have on the other person, are unable to appreciate that in this instance the person can see through it all only too clearly. He longs to say, 'John, old man, the fact is I haven't really got very long to live. I know there is nothing that anybody can do about it. I don't want to be a burden and I know it is not the kind of thing one ought to talk about, but I would so love to have just somebody with whom I could share it.' But either through consideration for others or simply because he is not sure what the reaction would be, he never says it. Like Oates who stole out of the Antarctic tent so as not to be a nuisance to the others, he is left to die alone and in the cold, not through lack of competent hands to nurse and care for him, but through absence of just one person who will share his dying with him.

There were a number at Le Court and St Teresa's whose families would confide in me that they had managed to keep the matter secret and that their relation or friend had no idea of their true state of health. I think they were all wrong. In almost every instance I am certain that the person did know. There is, moreover, the well-recorded instance of the man who broke down in front of a visiting social worker and said, 'I know that I have inoperable cancer, but my wife insists on pretending that all is well and I can't discuss it with her. The whole of our married life we've shared everything, but now when I need it most I can't share my dying.'

Again, I must be careful not to generalize. Every man's death is a death all of its own, different from anybody else's. One man is rushed to hospital, perhaps to an intensive care unit, where a number of strangers begin to battle for his life, so intent upon what they are doing that they may not even stop to ask if there is something he wants, or if indeed he wants the treatment at all. Another goes to one of the specialized homes where the emphasis is on helping him to die his own death in his own way, as free as possible from pain and suffering. Another will die in his own home amidst familiar surroundings and with his family there to share his dying with him. Not only is every death different from the others, but a man's attitude of mind will often change quite radically during the course of what we term his dying. Anger, envy, refusal to face the facts, disbelief, sadness are all emotions that may be felt and which have to be endured in preparation for final acceptance. It is of great importance not to belittle or pass over these emotions, but rather to try and put ourselves in the other person's position and help him to express them openly and fully. If it is unlikely that all of them will be felt by one individual, I think it is equally unlikely that none of them will be experienced. Clearly someone who has already reached old age, who has completed his duties, whose children have been successfully launched into the world and who can see a purpose and meaning to his life may be able to face the prospect of death peacefully and perhaps even with a sense of thankfulness.

I do not believe that any man can consistently look at death with equanimity. The Christian sees death both as a punishment for sin and as contradictory to his supernatural destiny – in short the last enemy to be overcome. It is impossible that no matter how great his faith or how holy his life he should not at some time feel an inner dread of death, the avenger. Wherever we find him, wherever situated either geographically or historically, man has always looked upon death as something from which to shrink, something distasteful. He always surrounds death with a ritual of some kind. Only when we see the stranglehold of death as having been overcome by the redemptive power of Christ's own death can our instinctive fear be replaced by hope. We may confidently assert, whether because of the strength of our faith or the fact that we see death as merely a sinking into oblivion, that we have no fear at all. But I personally find it very difficult to believe that this will prove to be the case when the moment of truth is actually upon us. In any event, what is fear but an occasion to prove our faith and our courage? I do not see why we should be afraid of acknowledging that we too will probably have a moment of dread and a feeling of desertion before we render up our soul.

My lasting impression, as I look back, is that each person, in his own personal way, underwent an inner struggle, at some stage during the process of dying. Many times have I puzzled over Arthur's strange words: 'I suppose that I shall have to go.' *Where* exactly did he mean? I have asked myself. Arthur was the perfect illustration of a man who had come to terms with his impending death, who looked towards it in the serene conviction that beyond its gates lay his eternal home in heaven. Yet when the moment was upon him, after a long period of some inner conversation, he looked puzzled and thoughtful and said, as if it were not at all what he had anticipated, 'Yes, I suppose I must go.' These were the words of a man who has been faced with a situation, or a choice, which he was not expecting, which required careful weighing up, and to which he could find no other response than agreement. With him, dying was not just an experience that he underwent passively. It involved both a positive decision and a positive act, and I cannot avoid the conclusion that neither was particularly easy. Yet after his eyes had finally closed in his last sleep a deep peace seemed to have entered the room.

In nearly every other case that I can recollect, I gained the same impression. Whatever may have been their circumstances or the form that their struggle took, they all finally died in peace. It was not, I am convinced, a peace of my own wishful thinking, but a peace that one could witness on their faces and that in some undefinable way could actually be felt. This cannot, I realize, always be true. Clearly it is not when a man dies in mortal agony, as in battle or as a result of some violent physical assault. Equally the outward appearance is deceptive when a person is heavily sedated or where his behaviour is affected by an unusually toxic disease. But, no matter what the exception, I believe that the general rule is true and it seems to me that the experience of those who have spent a large part of their lives in the care of the dying, and who have published their views and findings, bears the same testimony.

At the same time we must be careful not to draw conclusions which go beyond the competence of the available evidence, and which therefore may be misleading. A considerable amount of research has gone into the experience of people who have been pronounced medically dead and who have subsequently 'come back to life'. Although inevitably each story is different, nonetheless the majority appear to agree in two important respects. They report having sensed, or very often actually having seen, their loved ones who have predeceased them coming forward to welcome them. They also describe a sense of deep peace and well-being, and a longing to 'cross over the other side' to a place of great loveliness and beauty from which they are separated by some kind of divide.

On the basis of this evidence one could conclude that the process of dying, so far as its inner and spiritual content go, is nothing but happiness and light. However, none of these have crossed the true threshold of death; they have not passed over the 'divide' and can tell us nothing of what is involved in so doing. Their testimony is indeed valid, but only up to a point. One could equally well conclude that the welcome of their loved ones and the feeling of peace was needed in order to carry them through the ordeal of the crossing.

By the same token one can look at the peaceful expression of a dying man and conclude that his whole being is at peace. But in the same way that what we see on the surface of the ocean tells us nothing of what is happening at its most profound depth, so with a man who is asleep, or unconscious, or in the twilight between life and death. I once met somebody who was considered medically dead and who woke up to find a nurse standing over him with an expression of great wonder and surprise. She said that she had never seen anyone looking so peaceful, but according to him he had spent what felt like a night of intense struggle. Outside the window was a black, cloaked figure desperately trying to break in, while he endlessly shouted back, 'You can't come in here. You can't come in here.' He was convinced that it was the Devil, and could not comprehend the nurse's statement.

My point is that the expression of peace that we see, sometimes before death but usually afterwards, is the physical expression of the final, victorious outcome of death's inner struggle. The supreme act of faith that has brought it about, has lain too deep within the person's soul for any eye to see.

Yet even if this be disputed, what is beyond question is that a man's dying is transformed by the companionship and support of someone who is willing to identify with him and stand by his side as long as he is wanted. The knowledge of our willingness to do this, even if we are not actually in the room at the time, is a source of strength and hope far beyond anything that most of us ever imagine. My instinct, confirmed by what I have heard from others, is that even after a man has long lost consciousness he is still in some mysterious way aware of our presence, wanting us to remain, and very possibly still able to hear what we say. Never, under any conceivable circumstances, should we say or ask anything in his presence that we would consider an affront to his dignity were he conscious. We should uphold to the very last moment his self-respect, his right to share in any decision that affects him insofar as this is possible, and his human dignity.

There remains the other side of the story. To accompany a man on the final steps of his life as a companion and a friend, recognizing that it is his special hour in which we are privileged to share, is to receive as much as it is to give. It is to become more fulfilled and mature oneself, and almost certainly a little more sensitive to what is taking place in another person's heart. It is to learn how truly our living and our dying are part and parcel of the same process and how much easier it would all become if we could learn to talk about it during our lifetime as naturally and realistically as we do with life's other main turning points.

EPILOGUE

Like every traveller at the end of a long journey, I find myself filled with memories: many people each of whom in one way or another has either helped me on my way or enriched my life, or in some cases both. Only a very few of them have been described in these pages, but the others are present too, unseen and silent in the wings.

I have other memories as well, principally of a constant process of change. Change in the disabled person as he gradually adapts to his new situation and finally masters it; in my own evolving response to the problems and the challenge that confronted me; and in the movement of the public's attitude towards disability. It is there, also, in the steadily growing involvement of the State, and in the burgeoning of the voluntary agencies, each with a new and specialized role in helping disabled people towards a fuller and more independent life.

Wherever one has to do with people, one has to do with change. We forget this too easily. We forget that man lives in history, that man *is* history. We are fortunate to live in an age when the old static view of the world is disappearing, when the cosmos was pictured as having always been just as it was seen to be in the present moment. Instead we are coming to see that man is an integral part of the evolutionary process of the entire creation, and that whatever assertion we make about man needs to be taken in his historical context.

How many of us apply ourselves with all our mind and strength to designing and building a facility that meets some urgent need, and then, having successfully produced it, overlook the constant requirement to update and rethink so as to keep in step with an ever-changing society?

How many are quite content with the status quo, and far from seeing any reason for patiently working to change and improve it, look upon those who are trying to do so with suspicion and possibly even alarm?

In all such instances, and many more, there is a failure to realize that the world and society, just as every single individual, are still in a state of becoming, of striving towards ultimate perfection, a perfection that can only be achieved when the historical process has finally reached fulfilment. Unless we understand this, unless we all – passionately I feel tempted to say – believe in change, a change that leads to improvement and the gradual building of a better world, we are swimming against the tide of life. I offer three observations.

First, I believe that a charitable organization, like a religious one, gains a great advantage when it has slightly less money than it would like to have, and is at a disadvantage when it has more than it really needs. To be short of money, not quite able to see how you are going to make ends meet at the end of the month, is undoubtedly a source of considerable worry for those involved. At the same time, it is healthy. It means that you have to stop and think whether what you are planning to do is really necessary. If it is necessary, is there a cheaper way of doing the job? Can you take off your own coat and get down to the job of painting, or digging the foundations or making the curtains, instead of putting everything out to contract? Can you go out and collect bricks from this firm, tiles from that one, cement from another, and so on? You are put on your mettle. You feel challenged and compelled to leave no stone unturned to complete the work in the most economical way possible. In consequence, the whole organization acquires a new dynamism, and a reputation for doing what it can for itself instead of sitting back and asking for the moon, as is thought to be the case with some charitable bodies. On a much more profound level it also means that you are able only to do what the providence of God allows you. When you have the money to spare you can embark upon all kinds of ventures of your own choosing, and it could be that one of these will lead you off your true course, perhaps leaving you stranded at the very moment that a major challenge comes your way. When you are hard up you can undertake only what you clearly see is directed at you and you alone. History shows how even the religious orders, indeed even the Church herself, have lost something of their essential spirit and drive when they have become wealthy. So, I believe, also happens to the voluntary agencies – other perhaps than those whose sole function is to collect money to distribute to other organizations.

Money is certainly a major problem and one to which we must apply our minds with the greatest care. How are we going to collect what we need? How do we distribute it to the best advantage? Do we have the right to respond to any particular need, urgent though it clearly is, when we do not have enough in the bank? But, however great a problem money may be, most certainly it is not the first priority. The key to a successful Home, successful in the widest sense, is always people. Once you have the right people, even if only two or three to begin with, everything else including the money will follow. But not necessarily the other way round.

Secondly, it is possible to be so obsessed by what is wrong in society as to overlook what is right, and to think that the Golden Age is just around the corner if only we can turn the world upside down, and make others see things as we do. Far too many people who can pinpoint accurately and in dramatic terms what clearly needs to be changed, seem unable to recognize what is right and therefore to be retained, and are equally unable to tell us what form the new society should take. Perhaps they are looking solely at society itself and overlooking the reason for which society exists, namely people, and in consequence they fail to reach the heart of the matter. In order to bring about a truly just and free society, in which the dignity of man is upheld and each individual given the opportunity to fulfil his potential, it is in people first that the real change must come about. Man does not become good merely because the society in which he lives has been improved.

In the third place I hold that it is of the utmost importance that whoever embarks upon a social welfare or human rights project aimed at helping our fellow man or removing injustice, whilst giving himself heart and soul to his task and never losing sight of his ultimate goal, should not expect too much too soon. Time and time again, especially over the past twenty years, I have either known or read about people who have started with high and noble expectations, fired by great enthusiasm and idealism, and working away with all their strength for a period of years, only to discover that their early hopes have not been fulfilled as they anticipated. In consequence a great many, though by no means all, have slowly become discouraged, perhaps even disillusioned, and finally have given up and left the struggle to others. Had their leaders shown a little more realism and made it clear from the very start that the struggle would inevitably be a long one, possibly extending well beyond their lifetime, and that any advance, any victory, any change they could effect, however small, would constitute a real achievement, then things would have been different.

It goes without saying that campaigning for civil rights in an area of the world where widespread injustice is ranged against powerful political forces and social attitudes, is a totally different matter from working for a better deal for disabled people, and therefore generalizations are misleading. Nevertheless, whatever the particular objective may be, it is far better to start with the knowledge that we are human and as a consequence limited in what we can do, and that at the end of the day, for all our efforts, the results may not be very spectacular. I know of no substitute in any field of human endeavour for hard work, for clear and realistic thinking and planning, and, most important of all, for perseverance. The person who ferrets away, who never lets go, who, when faced with an impasse or just cannot see what he should do next, is content to wait and relax until something happens to give him an opening, is the one who will usually achieve the most. Without in any way renouncing the need to set our sights high, to be satisfied with nothing less than the best, and to commit ourselves totally and unreservedly to participating in the struggle to build a more liveable world, I have come to believe that the important thing is to keep going and to appreciate that even one small improvement is infinitely worth making. It is the multiplication of many people, each working in their own chosen field and in their own individual way that brings about genuine change.

But what of the disabled person, whose inner struggle and aspirations we have to some small extent been privileged to share? What of the man, or woman, whose handicap is so severe that he is in almost total dependence on other people's help? Are they only marginally contributors to the ascent of man towards our ultimate destiny? Or perhaps not a contributor at all? Or could it be that they have, each according to their particular circumstances, a unique contribution of their own? Could it be that by the very virtue of their disability, and correspondingly with its severity, they are in the forefront of our common struggle? We need to define what we mean by human achievement. Is the criterion by which we judge its value just the achievement itself? Or should we take into account the circumstances under which it was accomplished? Should we be content with the outward appearance, and let our gaze rest on the simple, tangible result? Or should we seek to look deeper to discover if behind what we see lies a hidden, still more significant reality?

Amongst the sayings of Christ as recorded by Mark is one, not so frequently explored, the full significance of which I find startling in the extreme. Christ was sitting in the Temple watching people putting money in the treasury, when, amongst the many rich, an old woman came up and put in just one penny. He called his disciples and, indicating that he had something of importance to tell them, said, 'This poor widow has put more in than all who have contributed to the treasury; for they have all put in from money they had over, but she from the little she had has put in everything she possessed, all she had to live on.'

This was not a parable, nor a saying that has a different

meaning when taken out of context; it was an unequivocal assertion clearly intended to be taken literally. What are we to make of it? We can, of course, deny that Christ knew what he was talking about, but those who accept his authority are forced to think about its implications. What we are being told is that in God's sight, and therefore in actual fact, the value of a gift is not in the size of the gift itself, but in what it has cost the giver. We would readily agree that more personal merit attaches to the one who in his giving has made the greater sacrifice, but to suggest that the penny of the widow is greater in actual value than the £10,000 of the millionaire is another matter altogether. Yet this is what we are being told.

Perhaps the solution will be simpler if we move away from the sore question of money. Suppose instead of the penny we look at some of those whose actions have figured in this book, at Lenny Dipsell for instance, who had so little in terms of opportunity and yet who achieved so much and made such an impact on the lives of those around him. There is the remarkable example, too, of Hilary Pole, MBE, who in her late teens became paralysed to the point where her only movement was in the big toe of her right foot. She was able to hear, but could not see, she could not breathe, she could not eat, nor move a single part of her body except that one big toe. Others might well have given up, but she was so determined to live, so utterly determined to put her life to some good use, that a specially designed electronic 'possum' was made for her, activated by a microswitch attached to her right foot, by means of which she could type. Being now able to communicate, she spent the rest of her life helping disabled people with advice and encouragement, organizing appeals to buy equipment for those who couldn't afford it, and making life more meaningful for those who came to see her.

Now that we are confronted with people rather than hard cash, our perspective changes. Our imagination begins to be fired by the way that somebody like Hilary is able to make so much out of so little, and we are less concerned with adding up what she achieved in absolute terms. If we were asked who we thought had achieved the most, someone in politics or Hilary Pole, we might well hesitate a moment before answering. What has happened is that the personal effort spills over into the achievement so that we have started to take into account the hidden, inner reality as well as the external, tangible result. We are on our way to equating achievement with the use to which a person has put his opportunities and his resources. Some of us at one end of the scale, contribute only out of what we have to spare, some, at the other end, whether out of their plenty or their little, give all that they have, even what they need to live on.

There are, of course, different levels at which we measure achievement. The person who, through physical fitness and personal courage, rescues a child from a burning house has clearly achieved more in terms of immediate, concrete results than another who tried his utmost but lacked the speed of action. But what I am talking about is achievement seen in the context of mankind's struggle to attain its eternal destiny.

As I reflect on the years I have so far spent amongst disabled people, I see them as men and women who are in the forefront of our common struggle, just as in a different way were those amongst whom I served during the war. I find unique the example they set of how to rise above adversity, of how to forget what might have been and concentrate on making the most of what is left. I find we need that example if we are to stop taking so much for granted, our good health and our many other blessings, and if we are to stop taking so seriously the little setbacks and the minor irritations of daily life.

We need a vision, a dream.

The vision should be the oneness, the essential and organic solidarity of the human family. The dream, that we each in our own way make our personal contribution towards building unity and peace among us.

The only question is how?

We tend to have confused ideas about peace. We talk about it, sing about it, demonstrate about it, but do we really think about it?

Peace is not just the absence of war or armed confrontation. Neither can a country living under a tyrannical and brutal régime be said to be living in peace. Peace is the effect, or consequence, of justice, just as conversely it is injustice – if under injustice we also include aggression against a sovereign state – that is the cause of war. We move towards peace proportionately as we succeed in removing injustice, particularly the injustice of mass starvation, and deprivation. Once we understand this, we have a clear target for which to aim. Whoever and wherever we may be, all of us can participate to some extent.

It is imperative that we recognize that peace through justice is the concern of us all, the concern of each individual person, each community, each political group, each nation. We must summon the collective will and the sense of urgency to face the task that confronts us and not rest until we have done all we can to complete it.

We will find that it is in going out to help someone whose need is greater than ours that we solve our own problems and become fulfilled as a person more fully the unique masterpiece that God wills us ultimately to be.